THE
COUNTER-INSURGENCY
MANUAL

By the same author

The Hostage Rescue Manual
Greenhill Military Manual:
Combat Shotguns
GI Series:
America's Commandos
Special Operations Forces of the Cold War

THE COUNTER-INSURGENCY MANUAL

TACTICS OF THE ANTI-GUERRILLA PROFESSIONALS

Leroy Thompson

**This Book Club Edition is Manufactured Under
License from Greenhill Books/Lionel Leventhal Limited, London**

The Counter-Insurgency Manual: Tactics of the Anti-Guerrilla Professionals
Greenhill Books, Lionel Leventhal Limited, Park House,
1 Russell Gardens, London NW11 9NN
and
Stackpole Books, 5067 Ritter Road, Mechanicsburg, PA 17055, USA

ISBN 0-7394-3076-9

Designed by Ian Penberthy

Printed in the USA

Contents

Preface

Although this work is described as a counter-insurgency warfare manual, it is important to bear in mind that rarely, if ever, has a counter-insurgency campaign been won strictly by waging war. Military action has an important role to play in overcoming guerrillas, but the philosophy espoused by the guerrillas must also be defeated, and this requires a well-reasoned combination of political reform, civic action and education of the population.

   In addition, it is absolutely essential that troops involved in counter-insurgency operations be well trained to differentiate between the population at large and guerrillas who may hide among the population. Counter-insurgency campaigns lend themselves particularly to atrocities if careful control is not exerted over troops carrying out military operations in close proximity to the civilian population. Often, the inability to tell friend from foe – or more correctly foe from neutral – can lead frustrated troops who are poorly trained and poorly led to slaughter innocent civilians on the assumption that they are guerrillas or guerrilla supporters. As a result, martyrs are created to the guerrilla cause and support for the government is eroded even more. To limit support for guerrillas and reduce the possibility of innocent members of the population suffering at their hands – or those of the security forces – it may be necessary to carry out massive population relocation programmes.

   During the decades immediately before and after World War II, many insurgencies came about through a nationalistic desire to be free of colonial stewardship. Among such campaigns were those in Indochina, Palestine, Algeria and Kenya. Others were attempts by

Marxist guerrillas to seize control of a country to install a Communist government. Cuba offers a good example of this type of campaign. Of course, after the Soviet invasion of Afghanistan, and in Mozambique and Angola, anti-Communist guerrilla wars have also been fought.

Today, very few colonial enclaves remain and, for the most part, Marxism is a discredited political philosophy. Nevertheless, guerrilla wars of varying intensity continue to rage in the Philippines, Sri Lanka and Colombia, to offer but a few examples. The line between guerrilla warfare and terrorism has also become somewhat blurred in cases where traditional ethnic or religious schisms have led to continuous fighting. In Israel, Northern Ireland and the former Yugoslavia, the old homily, 'One man's terrorist (or guerrilla) is another man's freedom fighter', has retained its validity. In Afghanistan, too, the War Against Terrorism waged by the USA, Great Britain, and their Afghan and other allies has begun to take on many aspects of a counter-insurgency campaign against remnants of the Taliban and Al-Qaeda.

Indeed, there are differences between guerrillas and terrorists. If Mao's classic paradigm for the successful guerrilla warrior is used, it can be seen that the true guerrilla cares about the population, which forms the 'sea' in which he must 'swim'. The terrorist, on the other hand, may claim to be fighting for an oppressed segment of society, but through the use of terror against civilians, he generally shows little concern about members of the population. At the beginning of this Preface, I mentioned that a counter-insurgency war cannot be won purely through military action. Political and civic action must be taken to remove civilian support from the guerrillas so that they may be defeated. In a counter-terrorist war, support for the terrorists may well come from states rather than a disenfranchised portion of the population – and draconian action may be called for against those states. In both counter-guerrilla warfare and counter-terrorist warfare, surgical strikes may have to be carried out by special-operations troops. Against terrorists, however, devastating military strikes are a must. Those who support terrorists should not be viewed in the same manner as members of the population who may offer at least some support to guerrillas, but who may be weaned away from them through an effective hearts-and-minds campaign.

Although there are some similarities between a counter-insurgency campaign and a counter-terrorist campaign, it is critical in the former to understand the goals and aspirations of the population to which the guerrillas appeal, while in the latter, it is necessary to take a much more direct approach without worrying too much about why the terrorists are terrorists. The critical requirements are to identify them, find them and eliminate them! Therefore, it is important to remember that this manual is intended to delineate the steps in a counter-guerrilla campaign, *not* a counter-terrorist campaign. That said, some actions and many tactics may be the same, and the same elite military units will often be involved. Certainly, an attempt must be made to convince those who support terrorism that the terrorists do not really represent their interests and may well be counter-productive in their attempts to achieve their goals and aspirations.

Guerrilla warfare has been employed successfully for thousands of years and, undoubtedly, will continue to be carried out in the future. Fortunately, the basic precepts of fighting a counter-guerrilla campaign have been proved successful time and again. The object of this manual is to present those precepts in a relatively concise and clear manner, and to offer historical examples to illustrate their effectiveness.

Leroy Thompson, St Louis, Missouri, 2002

Those who wage guerrilla war have been called guerrillas, insurgents, terrorists, bandits, freedom fighters, revolutionaries and anarchists, but this type of warfare has also been prosecuted by government agencies, such as the US Office of Strategic Services (OSS), British Special Operations Executive (SOE) and Special Air Service (SAS), Soviet Spetsnaz and special forces of various nations. Several definitions have been offered for guerrilla warfare, but Julian Paget's, in his book Counterinsurgency Operations: Techniques of Guerrilla Warfare, *is concise and to the point: 'a special form of warfare based on mobile tactics by small, lightly armed groups who harass their opponents rather than defeat them in open battle.'*

In US Special Forces manuals, the objects of directed guerrilla action are defined as:

1 Destroy or damage vital installations, equipment or supplies.

2 Capture supplies, equipment or important enemy personnel.

3 Divert enemy forces from other operations.

4 Create confusion and weaken the enemy's morale.

It should be borne in mind, however, that when special forces raise and direct guerrilla units or similar unconventional forces, those guerrillas are normally employed to support a conventional war. Guerrillas waging a true insurgency will be concentrating their efforts on destabilising a government, achieving the support of a population and gaining control of portions of a country.

In general, governments are faced

PRIMARY CAUSES OF AN INSURGENCY

with insurgencies because of a combination of factors – social, political, economic, military and psychological.

Among the social conditions that can encourage an insurgency are:

- contact with other cultures, leading to conflicts in traditional social structure and customs;
- pressure caused by urban and population expansion in an agrarian society;
- class, ethnic, religious or other rifts within the population;
- poor education or slanted education, as in some religious schools;
- an underclass that aspires to improved living conditions or has been led to expect a marked improvement in their situation.

Political factors include:

- a government out of touch with the aspirations of the population;
- corrupt or tyrannical leadership;
- domination by a colonial government or locally elected government supportive of the former colonial power;
- poor civil service system, inexperienced post-colonial leaders and/or an unstable government;
- poor communication between the government and the population;
- loss of government control of rural regions, leading to a lack of law and order;
- underemployed or frustrated educated class who advocate revolution;
- corrupt elections or otherwise ineffective political process;
- unwillingness of the government in power to tolerate opposition parties;
- a middle class struggling for political influence, but opposed by the right and the left.

Economic factors are almost always a contributory cause of insurgencies and include such issues as:

- endemic poverty;
- inequitable distribution of wealth;
- backward agricultural system, often based on a one-crop economy;
- inequitable system of land distribution;
- industry owned by foreign

companies or a small number of very wealthy locals;
- leaders incapable of developing a strong economy;
- inequitable taxation and tax collection, leaving the government underfunded, spending much of the country's wealth on the military;
- over-dependence on foreign capital;
- dependence on raw-material export or production of a single commodity;
- large-scale unemployment, affecting a substantial portion of the educated middle class;
- unstable currency;
- lack of natural resources or undeveloped natural resources;
- poor transportation and communication systems.

Military factors frequently help inspire an insurgency and, at the same time, make it difficult for a country to counter that insurgency.

Among the military factors that may contribute to an insurgency are:

- estrangement of the population from the armed forces;

- ineffective military and police forces that fail in their duty to protect the population;
- inappropriate or obsolete military organisation and doctrine;
- poor intelligence;
- power groups within the military with diverse allegiances;
- poorly motivated troops.

More subtle than the other contributory causes of an insurgency are a variety of psychological factors, including:

- nationalism;
- tribal loyalties that make it difficult to establish a sense of national identity;
- anti-colonialism;
- lack of identification by the populace with the government's goals;
- sense of injustice among a substantial portion of the population;
- lack of faith in the government;
- inability of the government to counter anti-government propaganda;

- low national morale;
- corrupt and/or unmotivated civil servants;
- sense of loss of a traditional way of life;
- anxiety about the national future;
- ingrained national taboos, caste systems or other traditional behaviour patterns that make economic or political growth difficult.

Currently, a perception that Western culture is eroding traditional Islamic values has led to potential insurgencies throughout the Islamic world, and to acts of terrorism against the United States and her allies.

GUERRILLAS THROUGH HISTORY

Although there is a tendency to think of guerrilla warfare as a twentieth-century phenomenon, the use of guerrillas as a force multiplier to allow less sophisticated groups to wage war against more advanced societies and armies can be traced to antiquity. For example, Alexander the Great found tough guerrilla forces in what is now Afghanistan, while Asiatic horse archers waged hit-and-run warfare against the Greeks and Romans. During his crossing of the Alps, Hannibal had to fight the ancestors of the Swiss, long proponents of guerrilla warfare in their mountains. Julius Caesar, anticipating many future generals faced with guerrillas, made good use of surrogate forces in Gaul and Britain to combat local armies.

In ancient China, Sun Tzu's *Art of War* expounded many precepts that later would be modified and adopted by other Asian proponents of guerrilla warfare, including Mao Tse-tung and Ho Chi Minh. Sun Tzu explained how the theory of *Chi* dictated the indirect attack and also showed how unconventional forces could be used in support of conventional armies.

The ancient Byzantines were among the best counter-guerrilla forces of the ancient world, making use of elite, mobile, highly trained professional soldiers to respond quickly to any threat from insurgents, while maintaining the best intelligence service of the time. The Byzantines were also expert at disinformation and at psychological operations designed to turn their enemies against each other. Occasionally they also used 'unconventional warfare' tactics themselves, based on the precepts in Nikephoros Phokas' *On Shadowing Warfare*.

Among the most feared warriors of the Middle Ages were the Mongols and Vikings, both proponents of hit-and-run tactics employing aspects of guerrilla warfare. Unable to defeat the English archer on the battlefields of the Hundred Years War, the French would eventually regain much of their lost territory through the use of guerrilla warfare.

COLONIAL WARS

British and French colonists in North America found the American Indian a master of guerrilla warfare, and soon learned to use the same hit-and-run tactics themselves. In the French and Indian War, Rogers' Rangers harried the French and established a long tradition of American special-operations forces that functioned much as guerrillas. During the American Revolution, American forces made extensive use of fieldcraft to wage unconventional warfare. Perhaps the most famous of the American guerrillas was Francis Marion, 'The Swamp Fox'. During this same period, Napoleon fared poorly against guerrilla forces in the Peninsula and Russia.

In the American Civil War, both sides employed guerrilla forces, although the South, being greatly outnumbered, placed more reliance on raiders, the most famous of whom was John S. Mosby. The USA continued to encounter guerrillas as it became involved in empire building during the late nineteenth century. After capturing the Philippines from the French, for example, US troops waged a counter-insurgency campaign against Moro guerrillas. Since US counter-terrorist formations are assisting Philippine forces against Islamic guerrillas in the Philippines as this is being written, more than a century later, this early American counter-insurgency foray takes on a new significance. Philippine guerrillas also proved particularly effective against the Japanese during World War II.

In 1896, the publication of Charles Callwell's *Small Wars, Their Principles and Practice* delineated the types of counter-insurgency or colonial war a major power might be required to carry out.

According to Callwell, small wars can be divided into:

1 Campaigns of conquest or annexation.
2 Campaigns to suppress insurrection.
3 Campaigns to avenge a wrong or overthrow an unjust government.

Note that the third definition is an effective description of the US campaign against the Taliban in Afghanistan. Callwell also analysed guerrilla tactics and offered suggestions to counter them.

Other works that addressed counter-insurgency warfare followed soon after. In 1898, Francis Younghusband published *Indian Frontier Warfare*, while in 1904, C. Miller Maguire's *Strategy and Tactics of Mountain Warfare* appeared. These works, along with *Frontier Warfare and Bush Fighting*, published in 1906 by the Adjutant General's Department in India, addressed counter-insurgencies in what are now Afghanistan and Pakistan, traditional arenas for guerrilla warfare. Another work, W.D. Bird's *Some Principles of Frontier Mountain Warfare*, followed in 1909.

At the dawn of the twentieth century, the Boers made use of their bushcraft and marksmanship to wage an effective guerrilla war against British forces in South Africa. In fact, the term 'commando' originated with Boer guerrillas. The French faced a guerrilla war in Algeria, which led to a century of counter-insurgency campaigns by the French Foreign Legion. During World War I, Pancho Villa engaged in guerrilla operations in Mexico, while Von Lettow-Vorbeck carried out one of the most effective guerrilla campaigns in history against far superior British forces in East Africa. T.E. Lawrence became legendary as Lawrence of Arabia during World War I, as well, rallying the Arabs to wage guerrilla war against the Turks.

TWENTIETH-CENTURY INSURGENCIES

Between World War I and World War II,

Mao Tse-tung developed his precepts of guerrilla warfare, which would become a textbook for many post-World War II insurgencies.

Among Mao's key precepts were:

1. Mass support.
2. Party organisation.
3. Military organisation.
4. Favourable terrain.
5. Economic strength.

During the same period, the British Royal Air Force was used in campaigns along the Northwest Frontier of India and in the Middle East to help pacify unruly tribes, using a technique known as air control, while the Russians pioneered the use of airborne forces against insurgents in Central Asia. The inter-war years also saw the US Marines gain experience in counter-guerrilla warfare in the various 'banana wars' in Latin America. The US Small Wars Manual was published in 1935, much of it based on the experiences in Nicaragua. In 1938, the Marine Corps, which normally found itself assigned to counter-insurgency operations when the United States became involved throughout the Western Hemisphere, also developed a 38-hour course in 'small wars' for its officers.

In his classic work, *Imperial Policing*, Charles Gwynn offered four precepts that would prove applicable in most counter-insurgency campaigns:

1. The civil power should remain paramount over the military power.
2. The minimum military force possible to accomplish the objective should be used.
3. Action must be taken in a firm and timely manner.
4. Civil and military authorities must co-operate.

World War II saw co-ordinated use of guerrillas in support of conventional forces. Russian partisans constantly harried stretched German supply lines in Russia, while the American OSS and British SOE supported resistance groups in France, Norway, Greece and other parts of Europe. The SAS, German Brandenburgers and other 'special forces' helped define a type of warfare that required highly trained military personnel to function much as guerrillas in the enemy rear.

The years following World War II saw guerrilla warfare become refined as a tool of Marxists attempting to exploit power vacuums left by the end of hostilities. The conquest of China by Mao Tse-tung's forces provided a staging area for Communist insurgencies throughout Asia, while the Soviet Union employed Communist insurgents as surrogates against the West in Africa and elsewhere. The French faced guerrilla wars in Indochina and Algeria; the British had to counter insurgencies in Malaya, Kenya, Aden, Oman and Borneo; the Americans took on the burden of fighting a guerrilla war in Vietnam, the loss of which was accompanied by Communist take-overs in Laos and Cambodia; Castro conquered Cuba; insurgencies raged in Greece and on Cyprus; many Latin American countries faced insurgencies, including Nicaragua, which fell to the Sandanistas; and insurgencies toppled white minority governments in Angola, Mozambique and Rhodesia (now Zimbabwe).

By the 1980s, however, at least some Communist governments were finding that guerrilla warfare could be used against Marxist as well as democratic and autocratic governments. The Soviets became bogged down in Afghanistan, and Communist governments in Mozambique and Angola faced their own guerrilla wars. In Nicaragua, the Sandanistas were threatened by the US supported Contras, while dissatisfaction with Communism seemed to create a fertile ground for insurgencies in several other parts of the world.

As this is being written, the United States' War on Terrorism in Afghanistan has taken on many aspects of a counter-insurgency operation, draconian military action being combined with a hearts-and-minds campaign and the use of local surrogates to defeat Al-Qaeda supported terrorists or guerrillas in many countries.

ESSENTIAL ASPECTS OF COUNTER-INSURGENCY OPERATIONS

Many lessons have been learned from more than a century of counter-insurgency warfare. Some of them will be explored in depth by this work, but it is worth mentioning some of the most important concepts to provide an overview. In counter-insurgency operations, commanders must be unorthodox and tactically flexible. It is important that they study other counter-insurgency campaigns, and learn from successes and failures. They must be willing to spend time and resources winning over the local population, and must be attuned to political as well as military realities. To support the military effort, an effective joint command-and-control structure has been proved crucial. Good junior officers are essential in pursuing a successful counter-insurgency campaign. Guerrillas must be kept on the run and deprived of secure bases. It is important to control food supplies and population to restrict the guerrillas' ability to re-supply themselves and recruit reinforcements. Counter-insurgency forces must be highly mobile and self-sufficient with the ability to gather good and timely intelligence. No matter how powerful or sophisticated the army, counter-insurgency warfare may have to be carried out at a very low-tech level with highly trained light infantrymen, often airborne, commando or special forces units.

The ability to act quickly in counter-guerrilla operations without long and obvious preparation for an operation is a necessity. In fact, guerrillas will watch for indications of impending counter-insurgency operations. These will include:

- weather that allows large-scale field operations (ie the end of the monsoon or, in mountainous areas, the melting of snow);
- arrival of a new commander for counter-insurgency forces, particularly one who has a reputation as an aggressive special-operations officer;

- change in the military situation that releases additional troops for counter-insurgency operations (*ie*

An important military step in fighting a counter-insurgency campaign is to train indigenous forces. In this case, US advisors work with Vietnamese Popular Forces troops. (*USMC*)

declaration that one area is secure, or a change of government in a neighbouring country, thus increasing border security);
- increase in the size of local garrisons and/or the arrival of fresh troops in an area. Also the deployment of helicopters or special-operations troops;

- increased patrolling or aerial reconnaissance carried out by counter-insurgency troops;
- increased intelligence efforts against guerrilla forces.

CIVIL DEFENCE UNITS

One of the most effective counter-insurgency techniques is to train local civil defence units to supplement anti-guerilla forces. Tactical training for these units will emphasise hunter-killer team operations, trail/border surveillance and interdiction, ambushing supply routes, raids against guerrilla bases and intelligence gathering.

Counter-guerrilla operations include:

1. Interdiction of supply routes and destruction of depots/stockpiles.
2. Capture of enemy equipment and key personnel.
3. Creation of confusion among guerrillas and lowering their morale.
4. Harrying guerrilla forces to keep them on the run.
5. Splitting insurgents into small groups and exterminating them.
6. Relieving villages from the threat of guerrilla action.
7. Denying insurgents the support of the local population.

CHAPTER 2

THEORIES OF INSURGENCY AND GUERRILLA WAR

To counter the guerrilla, one must first understand him. As a result, it is very important that those involved in counter-insurgency operations be familiar with the primary theorists of guerrilla warfare and their precepts. Of these, perhaps none has been as influential as Mao Tse-tung.

Although Mao's classic *Guerrilla Warfare* was not published until 1937, he had already developed some basic precepts that could be understood by the simple peasants who made up a substantial portion of the Chinese Communist Party by the late 1920s. His four simple tactical rules were:

1 If the enemy advances, retreat.
2 If the enemy halts, harass him.
3 If the enemy avoids battle, attack him.
4 If the enemy retreats, follow him.

Eventually, against the large, but inept, Chinese Nationalist Army of Chiang Kai-shek, these simple tactics proved highly effective. After Mao's 'Long March' of 6000 miles north to Shensi Province, the remaining nucleus of his guerrilla army had become toughened and shared a bond of hardship endured.

By 1937, Mao's theories of guerrilla warfare had been refined through experience in the field and many nights of thought, resulting in the publication of *Guerrilla Warfare*. Many of his basic ideas have been used again and again during the three-quarters of a century since they were published initially. Among Mao's most basic ideas were that mobile war and guerrilla war are complementary, and that in a protracted war, morale would prove the decisive factor. Mao also divided guerrilla warfare into three phases:

- **Phase 1,** during which the guerrillas would use hit-and-run tactics to capture weapons, would recruit and organise, and would liberate areas of the country from which they would operate.

- **Phase 2,** during which the guerrillas would establish a stalemate with their enemy; show the government's inability to function by attacking police and military outposts, and committing acts of sabotage, which would allow them to liberate more of the country to recruit more widely; and to train a conventional army in preparation for the final phase.
- **Phase 3,** during which the guerrillas would use powerful conventional forces to defeat the enemy in the field.

Different phases could take place at different times in different parts of the country. Most importantly, Mao understood that the aim of military action was to achieve a political goal.

THE BASIS FOR AN INSURGENCY

Many insurgencies that follow the pattern adopted by the Chinese People's Liberation Army (PLA) will be based on a party core, a mass civil organisation (including village militias, which function as part-time guerrilla units) and conventional military field forces.

The civil organisation performs multiple functions, especially during Phase 1 of an insurgency, among which are:

- Functions as an outwardly legitimate front, supposedly representing the population.
- Acts as an overt cover for the insurgency party core (NOTE: Sinn Fein in Northern Ireland and the Palestinian Authority are good examples of functions 1 and 2.).
- Helps mobilise popular support for guerrillas and against the government.
- Provides an overt means of social control.
- Develops a 'shadow' government, which may even win some seats in the ruling government.

Mao instilled a strong sense of self-discipline within the People's

Liberation Army, which stressed fair dealing with the local population, thus assuring their active or tacit support. Mao realised that the basic guerrilla organisation must remain simple and flexible. The PLA's primary unit was a squad that numbered between nine and eleven men. Two to four of these squads formed a platoon, two to four platoons a company, two to four companies a battalion, and two to four battalions a regiment.

According to Mao, guerrilla missions included:

- exterminating small enemy forces;
- harassing large enemy forces;
- attacking enemy lines of communication;
- establishing bases in the enemy rear;
- forcing the enemy to disperse his strength.

Mao drew at least some of his inspiration from the writings of Sun Tzu. He relied especially heavily on Sun Tzu's strategy of indirect approach.

AUTHOR'S NOTE
One of Mao's tactics, which has been widely used by other guerrilla forces, as well as many terrorist groups, is to attack an outpost, then ambush the relief force. Urban guerrillas often alter this precept slightly by planting a bomb, then leaving a second bomb designed to detonate while emergency services are dealing with the aftermath of the first.

STRATEGIC PRINCIPLES

Officers of Mao Tse-tung's People's Liberation Army had to learn ten strategic principles, which were basic to successful guerrilla operations:

1 Strike first at isolated, scattered groups of the enemy, then later strike at concentrated, powerful groups.
2 Take first the small, then the medium-sized towns and control the countryside, then later take the larger cities.
3 The primary objective is not to take and hold areas, but to destroy the enemy's fighting potential. Taking and holding cities or places results from

this destruction, but it may be necessary to fight many times before the cities are finally taken.

4. Always, in every battle, concentrate superior forces to encircle the enemy completely and annihilate him, letting none escape. If the conditions so indicate, strike the enemy with smashing blows by concentrating forces against his centre and one or both flanks, smashing him in parts so that our forces can be transferred to smash another part. Do not fight a battle of attrition unless gains outnumber losses. Though we may be inferior in numbers as a whole, we can achieve local superiority to win each campaign, eventually outnumbering the enemy and destroying him.

5. Do not fight unless you are well prepared, and do not fight unless you are sure of victory. Attempt to win every engagement.

6. Promote and reward bravery in battle. Do not fear sacrifice, fatigue or constant combat. Be willing to fight several engagements in succession with little rest.

7. Attempt to destroy the enemy while he is on the move, while still being willing to attack positions and seize strong points or bases from the enemy.

8. When attacking cities, seize those strong points and cities which are weakly defended or where circumstances allow it. Wait until strong enough and conditions are favourable, then seize the strongly defended cities.

9. Replenish our arms and manpower by capturing those of the enemy; men and material for our army are gained at the front.

10. Use the intervals between campaigns for rest, regrouping, retraining or training new troops, but such periods should not be too long because the enemy should not be allowed breathing space to recover.

PLA members also had to memorise eight reminders that governed their dealings with the local populace:

1. Be polite to the people.
2. Be fair in all dealings.
3. Return everything borrowed.
4. Pay for everything damaged.
5. Do not bully the people.
6. Do not damage crops.

7 Do not flirt with women.

8 Do not ill-treat prisoners.

These principles and reminders have proved themselves viable in guerrilla wars throughout the world; thus, understanding them is an essential aspect of countering any insurgency.

THE INFLUENCE OF MAO TSE-TUNG

Other Asian proponents of wars of national liberation owed much to Mao. For example, in 1953, the Indonesian Abdul Harris Nasutian published his *Fundamentals of Guerrilla Warfare*, which was strongly influenced by Mao's teachings. The greatest practitioners of Mao's style of warfare, however, were to be found in Southeast Asia. During the war in French Indochina, and later in the Vietnam War, Ho Chi Minh and Vo Nguyen Giap employed Mao's guerrilla warfare precepts, albeit with some slight modifications to fit their specific situation. That said, it should be noted that immediately after World War II

they made the mistake of moving too quickly towards Phase 3 and attempted open combat too soon, although when this strategy proved to be unsuccessful, Giap returned to guerrilla warfare.

Giap was a great believer in the three phases of guerrilla warfare – first, the formation of guerrilla bands, and the establishment of bases and safe areas; second, attacks on enemy communications and installations, and the establishment of control over villages; and third, the defeat of regular forces in open warfare. During the first phase, the Viet Minh employed a relatively passive resistance, intended to wear down the French while organising an effective fighting force. In his writings, Giap claimed to have moved into Phase 2 in 1947 with numerous guerrilla attacks and a stepped-up political campaign, aided by extensive propagandising. It was in 1950, however, after the Communist victory in China and the resulting availability of military aid, that the Viet Minh had access to more and heavier weapons with which to engage the French. Because of special considerations in Vietnam, the Viet Minh actually organised their forces into three groups or levels. There were main-force or regular Viet Minh units, regional units and popular forces. Regional units were based on zones, districts or provinces, while popular forces were village based. The latter merged with the population exceedingly well, since they maintained their positions as local farmers during the day, only carrying out guerrilla activities at night.

Ho Chi Minh developed his own equivalent of Mao's principles in his six acts that were forbidden to Viet Minh soldiers or officials, and six acts that were permitted and even encouraged:

Forbidden

1 Damaging land, crops, homes or belongings of villagers.
2 Attempting to buy, borrow or steal what the people do not want to give up.
3 Bringing living hens into the homes of mountain people (an example of violating local taboos).
4 Breaking one's word.
5 Offending people's faith or customs.
6 Acting or speaking in such a way that people believe the Viet Minh hold them in contempt.

Permitted and encouraged

1 Helping people in their daily work.
2 Purchasing commodities for those who live far from markets.
3 Telling interesting stories to the people about the 'resistance movement' (but not stories that give away important information).
4 Teaching the people to read and write and basic hygiene.
5 Studying local customs to better understand the people.
6 Showing the people that the Viet Minh are well disciplined, understanding and hard-working.

Most importantly, the Viet Minh and later the Viet Cong remained flexible. If defeated in the field, survivors would revert to guerrilla tactics while rebuilding their strength. Part of their flexibility arose from the loyalty of the peasants, who could be used to provide logistical support. Hordes of peasants carrying supplies kept the Viet Minh supplied, and at Dien Bien Phu even helped transport artillery to the heights above the French outpost. In simple terms, the strength of their convictions was matched by the strength of their backs. As in Mao's teachings, Giap believed that time was on the side of the guerrillas, and that temporary setbacks were minor events in a protracted guerrilla campaign. Against the French, and later the Americans, Communist guerrillas employed infiltration and ambush, often moving among the peasant population of Southeast Asia in the manner of 'fish in the sea', to use Mao's analogy. One important factor that is often forgotten when analysing the Indochina War is that while Ho Chi Minh and Nguyen Giap were Communists, they were also nationalists who garnered widespread support among large segments of the population. The Viet Minh were masters of propaganda as well, making great play of the French defeats during World War II, and they counted on the French to lack the resolve for a long colonial war so soon after that conflict.

The Viet Minh under Giap were particularly astute in carrying out raids against the French, choosing targets that offered potential for both military and political gains. For example, if they could defeat French troops, thus gaining both a political and military victory, plus capture weapons, a raid was considered highly successful. Viet Minh intelligence was excellent as well, since the population had been infiltrated so thoroughly. As a result, the French rarely made a move of which the Viet Minh were not aware well in advance. The Viet Minh were also masters at constructing underground bases, a practice that continued throughout the Vietnam War. Not only did these bases offer clandestine storage for arms and supplies without altering the landscape, but they were also safe from aerial surveillance and, in most cases, bombing. Even when a camp was discovered by the French, the Viet Minh were normally successful at breaking off action and escaping with negligible losses.

LATIN REVOLUTIONARIES

Although Fidel Castro and Che Guevara employed many of the tactics that had proved successful for Mao and Ho, they claimed that their brand of Latin revolution was entirely home-grown. Certainly, both Fidel and Che were believers in the value of propaganda in winning the support of the peasants. Also like Mao and Ho, Castro raided army posts, both for arms and for the propaganda value offered by such victories. Whenever possible, conscript soldiers were captured, then released so that they could extol Castro's concern for the people. As with many other guerrilla movements, Castro and Che made good use of the rough terrain of the mountains to develop a safe base of operations where their followers could exert control and gain self-sufficiency. In addition, Castro and Che were relatively astute in attacking economic targets, especially sugar mills in rural areas. Castro realised, too, that if he could remain a revolutionary force in being, the Batista government was so inept that it would continue to alienate substantial portions of the population, thus creating supporters for the revolution. Castro and Che did not have to fight large battles, but they did need to harass the Cuban Army, to lower its morale and to raise the morale of their guerrilla forces.

It was actually in retrospect that Castro and Guevara elucidated their Latin form of revolutionary warfare. In the latter's *Guerrilla Warfare*, Che established his philosophy of *foco insurreccional*, which held that smaller insurrections could precipitate larger ones. He argued that an insurrection in one province could spread to an entire country, then to neighbouring countries. Certainly the US government bought into the 'domino theory', which held that if one country in Southeast Asia fell under Communist control, others would follow.

Che set forth three rules for revolutionary movements:

1 Guerrillas or people's forces can defeat a conventional army.

2 Rather than waiting for optimum revolutionary conditions before striking, such conditions may be created by the revolution itself.

3 In Latin America, the primary struggle would be for the countryside.

Influenced by their success in Cuba, where the Sierra Maestra had offered them a secure base, Castro and Guevara believed that the Andes could be used as a centre to spread revolution throughout Latin America. In fact, when Che was hunted down and killed in Bolivia, he was attempting to establish such a base of operations.

Although other revolutionary movements had been highly dependent upon a charismatic leader as symbol of the revolution, Castro took this concept to the extreme and, hence, grew suspicious of Che, seeing him as a rival for power. Ironically, since for many during the radical 1960s Che was the symbol of the successful guerrilla, in Bolivia he forgot many of the basic tenets of guerrilla warfare, and ended up fighting in terrain that he did not know and depending upon peasants whose support he had not gained. Probably the greatest contribution to guerrilla warfare made by Che Guevara was the fact that he looked very good on revolutionary posters and made a good revolutionary martyr.

URBAN GUERRILLAS

Another Latin American revolutionary, who reflected the arrogance of middle-class members of the intelligentsia who became disaffected with governments and sought to foment revolution in the best interests of 'the people', was Carlos Marighela. In his *Handbook of Urban Guerrilla Warfare*, Marighela argued that by undertaking urban operations, a guerrilla force could draw security forces out of the countryside, thus allowing a traditional rural revolutionary movement to establish itself, at which point the urban and rural guerrillas would support each other. Marighela, who did not survive long after Che, sought to create a revolution, whether the people realised they wanted one or not. His primary method for creating the revolution was to employ a small group of committed urban guerrillas to commit acts of 'revolutionary violence', which would attract the attention of the population and gain their support. Such events would also cause the authorities to carry out acts of suppression, which would antagonise the population, thus making them more likely to support the guerrillas. Marighela put great stress on the importance of polarising the government from society to create revolutionary conditions. He felt that targets chosen by urban guerrillas should offer maximum psychological impact by discrediting the authorities and gaining publicity. Followers of Marighela's teachings generally have blurred the line between popular revolutionary movements and terrorism.

Although there have been other theorists of guerrilla warfare during the last half-century, most have built on the writings of Mao Tse-tung, at least to some extent. However, many have adjusted his basic tenets to fit the particular social or political situations in their own countries. By the final decades of the twentieth century, many of Mao's precepts were being implemented by anti-Communist guerrillas, rather than by Communist revolutionaries. Building on operations by the American OSS and British SOE during World War II, Western democracies have refined the use of guerrilla warfare as a force multiplier supported by special forces. Of course, as the military experts on guerrilla warfare, special forces units have also become the lead operators in counter-insurgency or counter-guerrilla warfare as well.

CHAPTER 3

GEOGRAPHICAL CONSIDERATIONS

Although a successful counter-insurgency campaign is dependent upon a wide variety of factors, geographical aspects of the area of operations can be extremely important in determining the success of the campaign and its duration. The more geographical features that favour the guerrilla, the more difficult the campaign.

An examination of guerrilla or partisan operations against the Germans during World War II offers a perfect example of the importance of geography. Rugged parts of Europe, such as Yugoslavia, Russia, Norway, and mountainous regions of France and Italy, offered fertile ground for resistance movements, while the flatlands of Holland and Belgium supported few significant resistance groups.

Among the most important geographical factors are:

- borders;
- terrain;
- climate;
- sea coast;
- population density;
- transportation network.

BORDERS

Guerrilla movements that can operate with impunity across borders or be re-supplied by a sympathetic regime, which shares a border with the country where they are operating, have a distinct advantage. During the Greek counter-insurgency war of 1946–9, Communist guerrillas enjoyed the support of friendly governments across the northern border in Albania, Yugoslavia and Bulgaria. The Viet Minh insurgency against the French received a major impetus when China fell to Mao, thus providing the Viet Minh with a safe haven for training and a ready source of supply. Whether the Al-Qaeda guerrillas operating in the latest Afghan conflict have been able to make effective use of the borders with Pakistan and Iran to retreat and regroup, prior to launching renewed attacks, remains to be seen. However, during the Afghan guerrilla war against the Soviets, Pakistan's Inter-Services Intelligence Agency (ISI) established training bases just within its borders, and by 1984 was training 1000 Mujahidin per month. Eventually, the ISI began sending three-man special-ops advisory teams into Afghanistan with the Mujahidin. By 1988, a total of 80,000 had been trained across the border in Pakistan. Unfortunately, the USA gave the ISI a virtual free hand in distributing aid, which resulted in fundamentalist guerrillas receiving

EXAMPLE

In Vietnam, throughout much of the war, the US attempted to fight a counter-guerrilla campaign, while the Viet Cong and North Vietnamese travelled back and forth across the borders with North Vietnam, Cambodia and Laos. Actually, the principal Communist re-supply route, the Ho Chi Minh Trail, ran just inside the borders of Cambodia and Laos.

most of it, assuring their strength following the Soviet pull-out. In fact, Osama Bin Laden initially became associated with Afghanistan in 1980, forming the Service Office for the Mujahidin to recruit 'holy warriors' throughout the Muslim world as well as to raise funds.

France's counter-insurgency war in Algeria was made more difficult by the safe havens offered to insurgents by neighbouring Tunisia and Morocco. Various other cases where a neighbouring country sympathetic to a guerrilla movement had an effect include Oman, Borneo and Nicaragua during the Contra campaign, but the value of cross-border support should be obvious.

UNSYMPATHETIC NEIGHBOURS

In other cases, a counter-insurgency campaign was aided by the lack of a sympathetic government on the border. In Palestine, for example, Jews fighting for independence from Britain after World War II lacked a sympathetic neighbour, although revelations about the Holocaust made it difficult for the British to fight a draconian counter-insurgency campaign against Jews seeking a homeland. In Malaya, although surviving elements of the Malayan Communist Party (MCP) did retreat to the Thai/Malayan border at one point, they received little assistance from Thailand and, hence, eventually were defeated. Although the Sandinistas

EXAMPLE

Rhodesia (now Zimbabwe) offers a classic lesson in the importance of neighbouring governments in a counter-guerrilla campaign. While the Portuguese were waging their own counter-guerrilla war in Mozambique and Angola, ZANU and ZANLA had far more difficulty in pursuing their guerrilla war within Rhodesia than they did once the Portuguese had pulled out and UNITA and FRELIMO took control of those former colonies. Of course, FRELIMO then had to mount its own counter-insurgency campaign against RENAMO, which was receiving support from the white government in South Africa.

initially waged a successful insurgency in Nicaragua, their Marxist government was surrounded by anti-Communist governments that later gave tacit, or active, support to the Contras, who waged a guerrilla war against them. In Greece, the KKE was much easier to defeat once Yugoslavia closed its borders to them in 1949.

Occasionally, it will prove advantageous for two governments to co-operate in counter-insurgency operations along a joint border. For example, once the French began to work with the Spanish to combat Basque terrorists/insurgents from the ETA, it became much more difficult for them to operate back and forth across the border.

COMBATING OUTSIDE SUPPORT

In attempting to counter the advantages of cross-border government support for a guerrilla movement, counter-insurgency forces can try various tactics. Political and economic pressure on the neighbouring country, or countries, offering support to guerrillas may sometimes reduce or eliminate that support. In some cases, military action in the form of cross-border operations against guerrillas in a neighbouring country may be threatened or carried out. US incursions into Laos and Cambodia to interdict NVA/VC (North Vietnamese Army/Viet Cong) supply lines and staging areas did restrict Communist offensive capability for a matter of months. Rhodesian cross-border actions, especially those carried out by the Selous Scouts, proved very effective at striking guerrillas in their 'safe areas', as did some SAS cross-border operations in Borneo. If the country fighting the counter-insurgency campaign is powerful enough, the threat of a naval blockade of countries supporting a guerrilla movement might also be effective. Against Indonesia, which was supporting Tentera Nasional Kalimantan Utara (TNKU) guerrillas and sending in its own Indonesian Border Terrorists (IBT), British forces launched cross-border CLARET operations, which accounted for a large number of Indonesian casualties.

EXAMPLE

One of the most successful cross-border counter-insurgency operations may have been carried out by the KGB or Soviet Spetsnaz in 1988, as the Soviets were beginning their pull-out from Afghanistan. Just prior to the withdrawal, the major Mujahidin logistical base in Pakistan was rocked by huge explosions caused by the detonation of 10,000 tons of weapons, including 30,000 rockets, stored there prior to distribution. The destruction of these weapons greatly diminished the Mujahidin's ability to harass the Soviet withdrawal, and also severely restricted their actions against the pro-Soviet Afghan government that was left in place. Although no proof was ever found that the explosions were caused by Soviet operators, the timing was so fortuitous that their culpability is generally accepted.

BORDER SURVEILLANCE

Another tactic that has proved effective in some cases is border surveillance, employing small, highly mobile units to gather intelligence and set ambushes. Such operations usually produce the best results if members of the local population who do not support the guerrillas can be recruited as border or trail watchers. The USA made good use of such units in Vietnam, as did the British in Borneo. The South Africans had a group of bushmen who acted as trackers along its borders and who achieved notable success against SWAPO guerrillas. Tribes with members on both sides of a border prove especially effective in counter-insurgency work if they can be recruited.

SEALING A BORDER

A tactic that has been used with varying results is sealing a border. Normally, if the border is relatively short, it can be sealed effectively. However, long borders will normally remain open in places. In Vietnam, the USA attempted to use technology to

High-tech methods are sometimes used in border security operations. This Air Delivered Seismic Detector (ADSID) was dropped along the Ho Chi Minh Trail to track NVA/VC supply lines. (*USAF*)

combat border incursions by 'seeding' thousands of electronic surveillance devices along the Ho Chi Minh Trail and elsewhere to detect NVA/VC movement. With the sophisticated satellite surveillance systems and other high-tech intelligence gathering methods now available, countries such as the USA can certainly make it more difficult for guerrillas to infiltrate

In Algeria, France achieved some success in sealing the border with Tunisia by establishing the Morice Line. Among its features were fortified blockhouses, barbed wire, minefields and electronic fences, and it made infiltration and smuggling supplies very difficult. The Morice Line proved especially effective at restricting arms smuggling; for example, in the seven months after the Morice Line was activated, 6000 ALN casualties were inflicted during attempted crossings and 4300 weapons were captured. France also established fortified positions along the Moroccan border for similar purposes.

commander of counter-insurgency forces may use the apparent disadvantage of a guerrilla-friendly border to destroy substantial portions of an insurgent force. In the War Against Terrorism in Afghanistan, for example, the USA has used its surveillance capabilities to locate groups of Al-Qaeda or Taliban attempting to cross the border with the tribal territories of Pakistan, then decimated them with air power, prior to mopping up with indigenous forces and special-operations troops. By forcing the enemy to run for a supposedly friendly border, then smashing them as they approach that border, counter-insurgency forces can gain both military and psychological victories.

SUPPORT FROM AFAR

Note that a government friendly to guerrillas can influence the campaign most directly if located on a border; however, it can still exert influence from afar. During the French counter-insurgency campaign in Algeria, for example, a combination of Communist Bloc and Muslim countries exerted

back and forth across borders, but even these advances cannot stop them completely.

A CREATIVE RESPONSE

Two important aspects of a counter-insurgency campaign are creativity and flexibility. As a result, the astute

EXAMPLE

When guerrillas are facing a country with far more sophisticated military hardware, a friendly power can also help to redress the balance. In Afghanistan, Soviet use of helicopters accounted for very high Mujahidin casualties until the USA supplied Stinger anti-aircraft missiles. Of course, a critical aspect of the US involvement in support of the Mujahidin was payback. The Soviets had supported the North Vietnamese against the USA in Vietnam, and US policy was to make the Soviets suffer as a result. This desire influenced the decision to allow the Afghans to have Stingers, some of which fell into the hands of Al-Qaeda and other terrorist groups after the end of the guerrilla war against the Soviet Union.

substantial influence in the United Nations against France. Many of these same states also supplied money, personnel or supplies to the ALN/FLN. Egypt, Iran, Syria, Saudi Arabia and Yugoslavia were particularly supportive.

TERRAIN

Physical features of the landscape can inhibit or enhance a counter-insurgency force's ability to carry out its mission. Inhospitable terrain, combined with a neighbouring country sympathetic to the insurgency, can make interdiction of movement very difficult. In Afghanistan, for example, the mountainous areas along the border with Pakistan and the tribal loyalties of those living in such areas have always made it easy for guerrillas to move from one country to the other. The jungle canopies in Southeast Asia and Latin America have also offered guerrillas freedom of movement across borders.

MOUNTAIN RETREATS

While the physical terrain along a border can be invaluable to insurgents, traditionally, for a guerrilla movement to flourish, it must have a relatively inaccessible base of operations. Although Cuba is an island, the Sierra Maestra mountains allowed Castro's forces to bide their time until they could move into the third phase of

guerrilla warfare. Mountains have also assisted other guerrilla/partisan movements, including those in Yugoslavia, Greece and Afghanistan. Ironically, the mountains of Greece, which traditionally have proved friendly to guerrillas, helped defeat the KKE when the guerrillas retreated to the mountains and attempted to hold

Air power can be used effectively against guerrillas if they can be located. (*USAF*)

them, thus surrendering their mobility. One of the greatest advantages of mountainous areas for guerrillas is that they reduce the effectiveness of air power and artillery. Even in the War on Terrorism in Afghanistan, US attack and transport helicopters have had difficulty in operating at higher altitudes. On the negative side for a guerrilla movement, mountains can be inhospitable and, unless a substantial portion of the population is sympathetic, re-supply can be difficult. In the War Against Terrorism, US and allied forces have on occasion actually attempted to drive Al-Qaeda and Taliban forces higher into the mountains during the winter, to restrict their mobility and allow their cave refuges to be attacked by air power, especially 'Warthog' aircraft, which can deliver massive firepower. However, because helicopters often have difficulty in operating at high altitudes, they are more easily brought down by surface-to-air missiles launched from nearby peaks.

THE IMPORTANCE OF TERRAIN SPECIALISTS

Just as Alexander the Great found when facing mountain tribesmen who waged partisan warfare against his forces, it is important to incorporate mountain specialists into counter-insurgency forces operating in the mountains. In the mountainous areas of Vietnam, the USA made good use of its Montagnard allies against the Viet Cong, and in Afghanistan, local tribesmen allied to the US forces have played a significant role in mountain operations. Specialised troops, such as the US 10th Mountain Division and British Royal Marine Commandos, trained in mountain and arctic warfare, have proved invaluable. In Latin American countries such as Peru and Colombia, which face insurgencies, specialised Andean troops are often invaluable, as are graduates of Colombia's Lancero School, which offers a Latin American equivalent of US Ranger training. The Lancero School is particularly effective at turning out troops capable of operating in the tropical rain forest, another region traditionally conducive to guerrilla operations.

TURNING THE TABLES

It is possible through careful planning to turn the advantages offered to guerrillas by the terrain into disadvantages. During the counter-insurgency campaign in the Dhofar area of Oman, the guerrillas initially enjoyed the advantage of operating in mountainous country served by virtually no roads. However, with the assistance of British advisors, the Omani government built roads so that troops and civic-action personnel could penetrate into the Jebel, then constructed a fortress line across the guerrilla supply routes, eventually starving them into submission.

PENETRATING THE FOREST

Jungles and rain forests have traditionally offered the advantage of

To practise their jungle stalking skills, members of the SAS in Malaya 'fought' each other using air guns and fencing masks. (*IWM*)

In Malaya, the British would often identify potential guerrilla areas of operation by spotting cultivated jungle clearings. To follow up on these sightings, Special Air Service 'Tree Jumpers' would parachute directly into the jungle canopy.

cover for guerrilla movements and operations. Even sophisticated counter-insurgency forces have found it difficult to penetrate the jungle canopy to identify the locations of guerrilla forces. Today, to an extent, US surveillance satellites allow detection of guerrilla operations beneath a forest or jungle canopy,

Left: A member of the SAS in Malaya prepares his kit for a 'tree jump' into the jungle. (*IWM*)

Facing page: A member of the SAS ready to carry out a 'tree jump' in Malaya. (*IWM*)

but movement is still less apparent than along open roads or trails.

One problem for guerrilla forces operating in heavily forested or jungle areas is self-sufficiency. For guerrillas to grow their own food, they need clearings, and these can be detected from the air.

In cases where guerrillas use the

jungle or rain forest as a haven, but are forced to rely on sympathetic portions of the population for supplies, counter-insurgency forces may either set ambushes along trails used for carrying supplies, or track those transporting them to the guerrillas.

WIDE OPEN SPACES

Deserts or arid plains offer the advantage of being inhospitable to counter-insurgency forces, but also make survival for guerrillas difficult, unless they have spent their entire lives in that environment. Such regions allow particularly effective helicopter operations, too. In eastern Angola, for example, the Portuguese found that guerrilla infiltrators were easily spotted from the air.

QUICK-REACTION FORCES

In cases where guerrillas use mountains, jungle, rain forest or other difficult terrain as a refuge, but regularly leave their haven to carry out operations, it may be possible to insert quick-reaction forces to block their retreat after an operation.

Members of the Rhodesian SAS on operations in Malaya. (*Rhodesian SAS*)

However, this is rarely successful unless the guerrillas launch an operation far from their safe areas. Generally, counter-insurgency forces will be more mobile than guerrillas, but to insert air-mobile or airborne forces quickly enough to be effective

EXAMPLE

In the Rhodesian counter-insurgency campaign, the Rhodesian Light Infantry became very skilled at parachute insertions, ahead of retreating guerrillas, to cut off cross-border retreats, but the terrain in Southern Africa, being relatively open, lends itself to this type of operation.

requires a very streamlined command-and-control system.

French troops made extensive use of helicopters during the counter-insurgency campaign in Algeria. (*ECP Army*)

ON HOME GROUND

Terrain can also favour the guerrilla if he is much more familiar with it than those carrying out counter-insurgency operations. In countless anti-guerrilla campaigns in Afghanistan spanning centuries, familiarity with every valley and cave has given the local tribesmen a great advantage. However, when a significant number of local counter-guerrilla forces are available, as in the War Against Terrorism in Afghanistan, a large portion of this advantage can be

Helicopters offer great mobility and versatility during counter-insurgency operations. (*US Army*)

nullified, especially if local forces are supplemented by highly trained special-operations personnel and air power.

CLIMATE

The climate of a region can play a very important role in the waging of a successful counter-insurgency campaign. For example, in tropical areas with a rainy season, both guerrilla movement and counter-

AUTHOR'S NOTE
One veteran special-ops NCO, who had taken part in numerous counter-insurgency operations, once commented to the author, 'If you're not pulling ticks off your ass, you're not chasing the guerrillas!'

insurgency operations may be impeded by monsoon rains, high winds or mud. In mountainous regions, heavy snows can affect movement by the guerrillas or security forces. Other aspects of climate can play a role in counter-insurgency operations. Tropical climates will allow guerrilla units to live more easily in the jungle and to survive without the need for fires, which can betray their positions to aircraft equipped with infra-red detectors. Generally, it will be easier to obtain food in a tropical climate as well. Tropical conditions may well inhibit operations by counter-insurgency forces if they are not acclimatised to the heat and humidity, and may contribute to a 'bunker mentality', since security forces will have a tendency to stay put in secure areas where it is more comfortable.

WINTER GAINS

Winter operations in mountainous regions require a willingness on the part of counter-insurgency forces to suffer discomfort to take the war to the guerrillas. Specially trained and specially equipped mountain troops are invaluable for such operations, since they can overcome much of the advantage guerrilla forces may have through familiarity with the area. The counter-insurgency campaign may actually make gains during the winter. This was the case with Soviet and allied forces in Afghanistan, as many of the Mujahidin would return to their homes for the winter.

PSYCHOLOGICAL EFFECTS OF CLIMATE

Climate may also have a bearing on the successful prosecution of a counter-insurgency campaign through its psychological effects on the local population and government. Generally, the more tropical the climate, the more likely indolence will be a problem, as slowness of action will have become a hereditary defence mechanism against the heat.

WATER SUPPLIES

An arid climate can have a distinct effect on both guerrilla and counter-guerrilla operations. When water is in short supply, guerrillas will need to secure access to a source when choosing a base. This will limit the search area for counter-insurgency forces. Arid areas will normally have little or no tree cover too, making it easier for counter-insurgency air-support elements to locate them. On the negative side for counter-insurgency operations, ensuring sufficient water for all personnel becomes an important factor in logistical planning.

SEA COAST

Just as a border with a country sympathetic to a guerrilla movement

EXAMPLE

In South Vietnam, the extensive sea coast combined with the rivers of the Mekong Delta provided the Viet Cong with waterborne supply routes covering thousands of miles. US SEAL and riverine operations made such operations costly in the Delta, especially after the Viet Cong infrastructure was targeted in that area by the Phoenix Program, but waterborne infiltration and supply were used by the Communists throughout the conflict.

South Vietnam's long sea coast was well patrolled, but there were still incursions, especially in I Corps, which was closest to North Vietnam. There were also insertions of Viet Cong and/or North Vietnamese frogmen at various times, in an attempt to disrupt the extensive US supply system, which was dependent upon major harbours. To meet this threat, the USA used of some of its best trained and most classified counter-insurgency forces – attack trained porpoises – which killed many of these guerrilla frogmen.

can hinder a counter-insurgency effort, so can a long sea coast, which will allow guerrillas to come and go in small boats, and make it easier to supply weapons and food to the insurgents. In some cases, an extensive river network may be used for guerrilla movements as well.

Island insurgencies normally face difficulties, since there are no borders across which guerrillas may retreat. However, islands are surrounded by the sea. When Castro returned to Cuba to launch his successful guerrilla war, he did so by sea, and at least some of his earliest arms shipments arrived in small boats, although many weapons were also captured from the Cuban Army. When the EOKA was carrying out its guerrilla war on Cyprus, the combination of an extensive sea coast and numerous sympathetic small-boat operators on the Greek mainland made re-supply by sea relatively easy. The British Royal Navy did have the assets to blockade the coast of Cyprus, but at that stage of the Cold War, and facing insurgencies elsewhere, Britain could never

allocate sufficient resources to seal the coast completely.

This is a geographical consideration

POPULATION DENSITY

that is only truly appreciated by serious students of guerrilla warfare. The ideal division of population within a country to support an insurgency would be at least seventy-five per cent rural, the urban population being restricted, in the main, to a few districts, often coastal. The large rural population is desirable to offer the guerrillas support and recruiting areas. Urban regions may also support a guerrilla movement of the Marighela model, and provide financial support and intelligence from a sympathetic, radical intelligentsia. Generally, however, the guerrillas will only move on the urban areas in the third phase of their campaign. If the population density is such that large rural areas, particularly with mountains, forests, jungles or deserts, do not exist, then normally guerrillas will have to opt for urban warfare. A perfect example is the Irish Republican Army (IRA), which has functioned primarily as an urban guerrilla movement throughout the conflict in Northern Ireland.

The EOKA on Cyprus, faced with the need to carry out more urban operations, placed 4578 bombs during the insurgency. Note that the IRA and other more urban guerrilla movements have relied heavily on bombs as well.

TRANSPORTATION NETWORK

The existence of extensive road and rail networks offers mixed advantages for both the guerrillas and counter-insurgency forces. Frequently, as demonstrated by the French in Indochina, a substantial road system will tempt security forces to rely on mechanised units and to stick to those roads. Such transportation networks also offer tempting targets for guerrillas, who can cut the tracks or roads at vital points, creating a substantial amount of confusion with minimal assets. A negative factor for guerrillas is that extensive rail and road systems allow counter-insurgency forces to move rapidly around the country. Generally, a small country with a relatively sophisticated transportation network is not appealing to the guerrilla. The EOKA found this to be the case in Cyprus, although that said, the guerrilla movement was surprising successful given the disadvantages it faced.

AIR SERVICES

Normally, the extent of air service within a country is not a major consideration in traditional guerrilla warfare, although the Al-Qaeda operations of 11 September 2001 certainly showed that terrorists can use commercial aircraft as weapons

EXAMPLE

Guerrillas in Rhodesia struck a massive psychological blow when they shot down an Air Rhodesia airliner in February 1979.

against a society and can cause far reaching disruption.

Certainly a guerrilla campaign cannot be won by sitting down with an atlas, but the astute counter-insurgency commander will pay careful attention to geographical and geopolitical factors when planning his campaign. The combination of good maps and, today, satellite photography, together with an understanding of guerrilla warfare, will enable the command staff in a counter-insurgency campaign to decide on the military assets required to fight the campaign, and to determine likely areas where guerrillas will establish bases.

CHAPTER 4

INTELLIGENCE AND PSYCHOLOGICAL OPERATIONS

To pursue a successful counter-insurgency campaign, timely intelligence about guerrillas and their intentions is an absolute necessity. In fact, the US Army's manual, Counterguerrilla Operations, FM31-16, states, 'Success in Counterguerrilla operations almost invariably goes to the force which receives timely information from the local population.' Equally important, however, are counter-intelligence measures that will deprive the guerrillas of information about counter-insurgency operations.

INTELLIGENCE GATHERING

Intelligence in counter-insurgency operations can be used to determine:

- causes of popular discontent;
- the strength and organisation of guerrilla forces;
- weather that can affect operations;
- terrain factors affecting operations;
- sympathies of the local population;
- identification of subversive elements;
- external support for guerrillas and sources of supply;
- location of guerrilla bases.

Actually, one of the first uses of intelligence is to determine whether or not an insurgency really is in its early stages.

Intelligence analysts will watch for the following indicators of an incipient insurgency:

1 Presence of trained insurgent leaders within the country.

2 Existence of underground insurgent organisations.

3 Insurgent attempts to create civil unrest and demonstrations.

4 Insurgent propaganda against the government and its policies.

5 Attempts to provoke the government into repressive measures.

6 Assassination or kidnapping of political figures, doctors, teachers, etc.

7 Guerrilla operations actually occurring.

8 School attendance declining.

Although some of these indicators may seem simplistic, it is often necessary for an intelligence service to convince the political leadership that there really is an insurgency; hence the need for clear-cut indicators.

FACTORS HINDERING INTELLIGENCE GATHERING

There are many factors that can hinder the gathering of intelligence for counter-insurgency operations. Some of these may be magnified if external forces are involved in counter-insurgency operations. In the War Against Terrorism in Afghanistan, for example, US and British intelligence personnel have been faced with the need always to weigh the agendas of various warlords in evaluating intelligence proffered by them.

The following hindrances to intelligence gathering will be encountered in many counter-insurgency operations:

- guerrilla penetration of government and security forces;
- corruption and/or inflexibility in government and security forces;
- no national identification system or census information to aid population control;
- government apathy, pettiness or active hindrance;
- poor infrastructure, making distribution of aid difficult (often combined with corruption);
- language problems;
- personality conflicts;
- lack of trained intelligence personnel;
- poor funding and material support;
- poor supervision or guidance of local intelligence assets;
- political factionalism;
- excessively centralised authority;
- local population's fear of insurgents.

Many military units that specialise in counter-insurgency warfare, such as the British SAS and US Army Special Forces, include personnel who have been trained in developing local intelligence assets and gathering intelligence that is specifically useful for counter-insurgency operations. Finding minority populations or others in guerrilla areas of operation who do not support the guerrillas will often provide fertile sources of intelligence.

PRECAUTIONS TAKEN BY GUERRILLAS

Another difficulty in gathering intelligence will generally be the precautions guerrillas take to limit information about themselves. These will include carefully screening members and, perhaps, the use in certain cultures – as with the Mau Mau in Kenya during the 1950s – of complex oath-taking ceremonies. To discourage traitors, many guerrilla units will kill turncoats in a particularly gruesome fashion. The IRA's 'creative' use of power drills on the kneecaps of suspected informers has served as a grisly warning as well.

Guerrillas will also use many of the same counter-intelligence methods as the security forces, including restricting information given to the local population, planting false intelligence and carrying out deception operations. For virtually every guerrilla group, infiltration of government intelligence and security agencies remains a high priority.

SOURCES OF INTELLIGENCE

Sources of intelligence useful in counter-insurgency operations include:

- undercover agents;
- civil government agencies and personnel;
- analysis of guerrilla activity;
- captured personnel, documents and equipment;
- timely and applicable studies;
- maps and photographs;
- guerrilla publications;
- members of the population;
- guerrilla communications intercepts

EXAMPLE

Oaths taken by the Mau Mau

- If I ever reveal the secrets of this organisation, may this oath kill me.
- If I ever sell or dispose of any Kikuyu land to a foreigner, may this oath kill me.
- If I ever fail to follow our great leader Kenyatta, may this oath kill me.
- If I ever inform against any member of this organisation or against any member who steals from a European, may this oath kill me.
- If I ever fail to pay the fees of this organisation, may this oath kill me.
- If I am sent to bring in the head of an enemy and I fail to do so, may this oath kill me.
- If I fail to steal anything I can from a European, may this oath kill me.
- If I know of any enemy to our organisation and I fail to report him to my leader, may this oath kill me.
- If I am ever sent by a leader to do something for the house of Kikuyu and I refuse, may this oath kill me.
- If I refuse to help in driving the Europeans from this country, may this oath kill me.
- If I worship any leader but Jomo Kenyatta, may this oath kill me.
- If I am called upon to do so, may this oath kill me, with four others I will kill a European.
- I will kill a Kikuyu who is against the Mau Mau, even if it be my mother or father, or brother or sister, or wife or child.
- I will help dispose of the body of a murdered person so that it may not be found.
- I will never disobey the leaders of this society.

(Many guerrilla organisations have relied on written messages in the past, while some Marxist movements actually encouraged members to keep diaries, which were often treasure troves of information. Today, guerrillas commonly use mobile phones, computers and other high-tech communications devices. As a

result, technical intelligence personnel are essential.);
- local police intelligence sources.

ESSENTIAL INFORMATION

Once sources of intelligence have been developed, information should be sought and obtained about the following:

- local terrain (it is amazing how often maps of guerrilla areas of operations are inaccurate or non-existent);
- ideology of the local population and degree of support for the guerrillas;
- logistical support available to the guerrillas in the area;
- potential guerrilla targets;
- identification of guerrillas;
- guerrilla tactics and techniques, especially when committing sabotage and carrying out espionage;
- guerrilla psy-ops/propaganda and their success.

EFFECTIVE USE OF INTELLIGENCE

Simply gathering intelligence is generally not sufficient to win a counter-insurgency campaign. The intelligence must be employed in a timely manner.

These five steps allow intelligence to be used effectively:

1 Develop a plan for collection.
2 Carry out the actual collection.
3 Process the data.
4 Disseminate the intelligence.
5 Employ the intelligence on counter-guerrilla operations.

Often, Step 3, processing, is very difficult if there are not enough trained linguists to translate guerrilla documents, or if the volume of raw intelligence is too large. By 1968, for example, three million pages of enemy documents were arriving at the Military Assistance Command Vietnam Intelligence Center every month!

To use the intelligence gathered,

analysts must watch for indicators that point to certain guerrilla activities.

The following indicators might point to an impending attack on a village or installation:

- propaganda in the form of 'educational' lectures near the village or installation;
- increasing guerrilla activity and patrolling in the area;
- ambushes of local security patrols;
- indicators that insurgent forces are on the move in the area;
- threats of attack and propaganda directed towards the village or installation;
- kidnapping or murder of local leaders;
- rumours of impending attack.

The following indicators may point to a specific village being sympathetic to the insurgents:

- freedom of movement for villagers;
- no security deemed necessary for village farm workers when working in the fields;

EXAMPLE

In Malaya, where food denial measures were extremely effective, British intelligence personnel often watched villagers suspected of having guerrilla sympathies to see if they were smuggling food to the insurgents. Once a smuggler had been identified, he was given the choice of continuing to smuggle food, but to act as an informant, or to be placed in a detention facility. A large number of very effective informants were gained in this manner.

- obvious lack of fear of the guerrillas;
- village and villagers immune from guerrilla attack, or if attacked the action appears to have been a ruse;
- trails from village to known guerrilla base areas.

Indicators that point to an area as being a guerrilla base:

- designed to be concealed from aerial reconnaissance;
- designed to allow observation of

points of approach;
- designed to be difficult to reach, but easy to defend;
- designed with routes for easy withdrawal;
- natural water supply nearby;
- placed near settlements or other potential targets.

To ambush guerrillas as they infiltrate an area, it is important to identity infiltration routes and rest areas along those routes.

Indicators of a guerrilla infiltration route include:

- crops growing in areas away from villages, or food caches away from villages;
- trails located away from populated areas, especially when there are markers that indicate use by non-locals;
- abandoned campsites;
- water supply near the trails;
- abundant game, especially if snares or traps not set by local hunters are found;
- frequent, but transitory, sightings of

enemy units in the area;
- trails that have not been booby-trapped;
- no combat action near the trails;
- smoke from campfires.

One of the most important uses of intelligence is to determine the effectiveness of the counter-insurgency campaign:

Indicators to determine the effectiveness of a counter-insurgency campaign:

- amount of country under the control of government forces;
- casualties;
- morale;
- relative defection rates from guerrillas and government forces;
- labour unrest, including frequency of strikes;
- standard of living;
- intelligence provided voluntarily by the population;
- relative military strength;
- insurgent attacks, assassinations and kidnapping increasing or declining;

DRAWING CONCLUSIONS

- effectiveness of tax collecting.

In many cases, the indicators may be incorporated into checklists to assist analysts in spotting trends in guerrilla activity. It is also very useful to study successful and unsuccessful counter-insurgency campaigns to determine key factors of which intelligence operatives must be aware. For example, it is generally accepted that the Mau Mau insurgency in Kenya failed due to five primary factors:

1 Lack of strategy and coherent
2 objectives.
3 Inadequate weaponry.
4 Poor leadership.
5 Lack of external support and advice.

Inability to retain the loyalty of the population, especially the Kikuyu tribe from which the Mau Mau recruited.

By examining these factors, and those that determined the outcome of other counter-insurgency campaigns, the intelligence specialist should be able to draw conclusions about the success or failure of the campaign in which he or she is involved. It is important, as well, to maintain the focus of the intelligence effort.

EXAMPLE

In the counter-insurgency campaign in Cuba, Batista's intelligence service was more concerned with countering potential coups from within the government or armed forces than with gathering intelligence on Castro and his supporters. This lack of focus contributed to Castro's successful conquest of Cuba.

IDENTIFYING AND DETAINING GUERRILLAS

Using intelligence to determine what appeal a guerrilla movement has for the population and attempting to take action to win the population away from the guerrillas are important, as are psychological operations to counteract guerrilla propaganda. However, an extremely valuable use of intelligence is the identification and detention of members of the guerrilla force.

Among intelligence measures that can further the identification and detention mission are:

- background checks on members of the population;
- surveillance of known guerrillas to identify sympathisers and safe houses;
- setting ambushes and booby-traps in guerrilla areas of operation;
- use of skilled trackers and tracker dogs;
- clearing of vegetation to allow aerial surveillance;
- use of electronic detection devices;
- monitoring of communications systems;
- installation of checkpoints and carrying out of searches;
- resettlement of villages suspected of guerrilla sympathies;
- distribution of photographs and handbills detailing known guerrillas;
- offering rewards for information leading to the capture of guerrillas;
- periodically photographing members of each village for later comparison to determine who is entering and leaving the area;
- issuing of photographic identification cards to the population in the area of operations.

Note that control measures, such as monitoring telephone calls and extensive use of checkpoints, can be quite effective in inhibiting guerrilla communications and movement. On the other hand, such infringements of civil liberties may well cause large segments of the population, who would normally remain neutral during an insurgency, to become resentful of the government and tacitly, if not actively, support the guerrillas. Draconian measures by the French in Algeria often had this effect. Consequently, it is preferable only to implement some measures in areas where the guerrillas are already exerting a strong influence. This is one reason why determining which portions of the population support the guerrillas is an important goal of the

DIRECT ACTION

intelligence gathering effort.
In some cases, intelligence operations can become much more 'hands on'. US CIA and special-ops personnel used direct action in Vietnam during the Phoenix Program to eliminate the Viet Cong infrastructure; 'Nenita' units assassinated Huk leaders in the Philippines; and KGB Alpha teams were used to eliminate troublesome insurgents from time to time.

WIDE-RANGING SOURCES OF INTELLIGENCE

EXAMPLE During the counter-insurgency campaign in Algeria, SDECE (Service de Documentation Extérieur et de Contre-espionage) employed its Action Service to target and eliminate ALN leaders inside and outside the country. An Action Service special-ops unit, the Groupement Légère d'Intervention (GLI), operated under the cover of being a signals unit composed of French reservists. The unit booby-trapped a radio transmitter so that it would explode when turned on, then allowed it to be captured by the guerrillas. It killed four high-ranking members of the ALN.

A strong counter-insurgency intelligence effort will make use of as many sources as possible. Good relationships with civil-affairs personnel, who work closely with the population, and with local police should be cultivated, as both can be excellent sources of intelligence. It is also important that personnel engaged in counter-insurgency operations receive more detailed briefings than might be necessary for more traditional military operations. Knowledge of local customs, geography, religion, history, ethnic make-up and similar information can allow counter-insurgency personnel to function much more effectively among the population. The intelligence effort should devote substantial resources to studying enemy propaganda and appeals to the people. Once these are understood, psychological operations may be undertaken to counter them. As a result of the importance of intelligence in counter-insurgency operations, counter-insurgency forces will normally require a greater number of intelligence specialists than a traditional military force of similar size.

PSYCHOLOGICAL OPERATIONS

In the context of counter-insurgency warfare, psychological operations are intended to convince members of the population to support the government rather than the guerrillas, to help identify guerrillas and to separate the guerrillas from the population. Additional benefits of psychological operations are that segments of the population may be convinced to offer active support to a counter-insurgency campaign by taking up arms as local military formations, and that less committed guerrillas may actually turn

themselves in.

UNDERSTANDING THE POPULATION

For psychological operations to be effective, it is absolutely essential to understand the population. For example, in Muslim countries, psychological actions against Marxist guerrillas frequently have emphasised the fact that Communism is 'godless'.

When employing psychological techniques in a counter-insurgency campaign, it has normally been most effective to:

- use an indirect approach to change less strongly held views first, then more strongly held ones;
- use a variety of approaches to appeal to different segments of the population;
- use group identification techniques to convince a population to support the counter-insurgency effort. To accomplish such group identification, psy-ops may play upon religious beliefs, loyalty to a popular ruler, patriotism or other

British psy-ops personnel did an especially effective job in Malaya when MCP guerrillas began slashing the rubber trees upon which employment for large numbers of Malays depended. As a result, Malays were exhorted to turn against those who broke 'their brothers' rice bowls'. Ironically, however, the damage done actually drove up tin and rubber prices in Malaya, thus bringing in more money for the counter-insurgency campaign.

feelings.

One of the most useful aspects of psychological operations is to convince a population that hardships imposed due to a counter-insurgency campaign – such as checkpoints, curfews and other alterations in lifestyle – should be blamed on the guerrillas rather than the government.

UNDERSTANDING GUERRILLA PROPAGANDA

An important step in employing psychological techniques is understanding guerrilla propaganda and its effectiveness. US psy-ops personnel have used the SCAME formula to analyse guerrilla propaganda:

- **S**ource
- **C**ontent
- **A**udience
- **M**edia
- **E**ffects

Counter-propaganda operations directed against guerrillas will include denial operations, such as jamming their radio broadcasts and confiscating printed materials, but active counter-propaganda efforts designed to disprove guerrilla claims and enhance the image of the government will be employed as well. Frequently, an important step in countering guerrilla propaganda is convincing government employees to be more concerned about how they are perceived when dealing with the population, especially the poorer classes who are likely to be most susceptible to guerrilla blandishments.

CREATING A SENSE OF NATIONAL IDENTITY

One of the most beneficial types of psychological operation is a scheme that helps the population to develop a sense of national identity.

Actions that may be undertaken to establish a sense of national identity include:

- satisfy individuals' psychological goals (*ie* make a better life for themselves and their families);
- give members of the population a sense of prestige;
- build a sense of belonging;
- develop a sense of equity (*ie* avoid the appearance of favouring individuals or particular population groups because of their class or ethnic origin);
- give timely, honest explanations of the situation and the pursuit of the counter-insurgency campaign;
- develop a sense of working together to achieve successes;

EXAMPLE

Attempts to build a national identity can fail if those carrying out the psychological operations don't really understand their target group. In Algeria, psy-ops stressed 'integration', whereby all Algerians would be subjects of France. They also indicated that the French Army would never leave Algeria. For Algerian Muslims, who had suffered years of economic, legal and racial discrimination from the *colons* (French colonists), these messages only hardened the resolve of the members of the FLN, who did not want to be part of France, which they viewed as an occupying colonial power. Exacerbating this situation was the fact that the French Army and the French government were pursuing different agendas in Algeria, a situation that eventually resulted in a revolt by a portion of the French Army, led by the members of the 1st Foreign Legion Parachute Regiment.

In Malaya, British psy-ops personnel realised that a substantial portion of the basis for the insurgency lay in the hostility between Malay and Chinese sections of the population. By emphasising that the British intended to leave Malaya and give the Malays self-government, but that they would make sure the Chinese were integrated into the political process, a substantial number of those supporting the Malaysian Communist Party (MCP) were enticed away. In an attempt to address the lack of appeal his movement held for the Malaysian population, Chen Ping, the leader of the MCP, changed its name to the Malaysian Races Liberation Army in 1949, but ninety per cent of his support remained among the Chinese minority.

- instil a national sense of purpose.

GAINING THE SUPPORT OF THE POPULATION

When attempting to gain the support of a population, themes to stress include:

- government programmes are helping the population – point out successes (Note that many peasants cannot understand long-term projects, such as dams that will come on line in a decade, but need to see simpler programmes that affect them directly.);
- problems can be solved through negotiation and elections;
- guerrilla operations are futile and costly;
- guerrillas are actually under the control of external forces;
- many guerrilla leaders are really bandits preying on the people for whom, allegedly, they are fighting;
- population and resource controls are necessary measures (Normally, it is important that villagers who are moved as part of a population control effort do not find themselves worse off than before, with less-fertile land or in a location farther from water.);
- much guerrilla ideology contains

flawed logic;

- external countries, which are helping the guerrillas, are doing the population a disservice.

In deciding on the types of psy-ops that will be most effective in counter-insurgency warfare, it is necessary to consider various aspects of the target population. The people's susceptibility to such operations should be analysed, as should their attitudes and value systems; their access to different types of media and the effects these have; and special themes or symbols that hold particular significance.

THE TRUTH AND BLACK OPS

Normally, in psychological operations designed to win over a population, being truthful is desirable to give the government and security forces credibility. However, this does not preclude 'black operations' designed to alienate the population from the guerrillas. For example, planting a false

EXAMPLE A good example of how psy-ops based on lies can backfire occurred in Cuba when the Batista government broadcast that Castro had been killed during his landing on Cuba. Once this had been established as an obvious lie, the Batista government was discredited and Castro's prestige

guerrilla manual with a section on seducing local girls or setting forth techniques for torturing village leaders might be an effective black-op. Especially productive have been black-ops designed to convince guerrilla groups that they have been infiltrated by spies from the security forces, often resulting in a substantial number of loyal guerrillas being killed and mistrust being sewn among the remainder. This technique has been used quite effectively by British Intelligence against the IRA. In fact, psy-ops should not only be directed at the population in general, but also at the insurgents, especially those at the lower level or those who are least committed.

Appeals that separate guerrillas from their leaders can be very effective in bringing in defectors. Combined with a re-education programme that allows former guerrillas to be re-integrated into society, or even to fight against their former comrades, a psy-op offering amnesties and rewards for turning in leaders, offering intelligence or surrendering arms can be extremely productive.

Among the counter-insurgency campaigns that have made good use of amnesties are:

- Greece, where in September 1947 alone, 4000 guerrillas surrendered;
- The Philippines, where prisoners were treated well so that word would filter out to other guerrillas;
- Kenya, where a re-integration programme stressed confession of sins, hard labour, re-education and participation in sports.

Black propaganda directed against guerrillas might employ some of the following methods:

- **Gossip or rumour.** By planting rumours, either among the population or guerrilla units, that lower guerrilla morale, less committed sympathisers may be weaned away from the insurgents. For example, rumours could be planted among guerrilla fighters to suggest that those seriously injured in combat are being eliminated because they are too much trouble.
- **Pornography.** It is human nature, especially among males, to look at pornography. This can be employed to denigrate guerrilla leaders, or depict them with young girls or boys, etc.
- **Jokes or witticisms.** Jokes are one of the most effective forms of black propaganda and can be effective in playing upon basic fears or prejudices.
- **Slogans.** Slogans that are allegedly those of the guerrillas, but which contain themes abhorrent to many members of the insurgency, can be quite effective (*ie* in an Islamic insurgency, 'The party is the only god!').
- **Counterfeit currency.** If counterfeit

currency can be slipped into guerrilla hands, they become discredited among those with whom they spend it when those people are detained for passing the counterfeit money.

- **Poison-pen letters.** For example, letters ostensibly from one guerrilla leader to another's subordinate, criticising the superior, can help sew disharmony.
- **Representing the voice of the enemy.** Radio broadcasts purporting to be from a guerrilla radio station can be very effective at lowering morale. Such broadcasts, for example, might attempt to justify a supposed massacre of guerrilla fighters by their officers.

DISSEMINATING THE MESSAGE

Getting information out to what is, in many cases, a rural and relatively unsophisticated population is an important part of psy-ops.

Today, the use of video tapes for psychological operations is quite effective, as are simple printed materials

EXAMPLE During the British counter-insurgency campaign in Dhofar, inexpensive transistor radios were made available to residents of the Jebel, but the radios were so designed that only pro-government broadcasts were likely to be received. At first, the radios were given gratis, but the guerrillas kept confiscating them. However, once the radios were placed on sale in the bazaar at a low price, those owning them had a vested interest in concealing them from the guerrillas.

with lots of illustrations. Psy-ops materials combined with civic action may also be effective. If, for example, agricultural products – seeds, animal feed, etc – are supplied to rural peasants, their packaging can carry pictorial pro-government messages.

DENYING GUERRILLAS INFORMATION

Counter-intelligence measures to deny

guerrillas information about counter-insurgency operations are as important as the gathering of intelligence. Among the measures that have proved effective are:

- restricting civilian communication and movement within the area of operations for the duration of the counter-insurgency action;
- briefing all personnel on guerrilla intelligence operational techniques and counter-measures;
- disposing of all documents and rubbish in a secure manner;
- using passwords for admittance to installations;
- avoiding contact by reconnaissance personnel operating in an area prior to the launching of an operation or, if contact is made, employing suppressed weapons to eliminate guerrillas quietly;
- not changing routine, thus telegraphing impending operations;
- maintaining security about logistical planning;
- carrying out troop movements under cover of darkness, bad weather, etc, and moving as quickly as possible;

- being careful in communications, since the enemy may have captured radios;
- carrying out deception operations to confuse guerrillas about where an operation will really be launched;
- keeping the identities of intelligence agents secret to avoid assassination.

EXAMPLE

The importance of deception cannot be overemphasised. In Malaya, for example, British forces would very obviously prepare for a sporting event apparently involving a significant number of troops, but then leave only a small number to simulate the match while others were deployed on a sweep of a guerrilla operating area.

Planting false intelligence can be very useful. The French intelligence service, for example, made excellent use of turned guerrillas in Algeria to pass on disinformation. In Afghanistan, so riddled with informers were the Afghan government forces that, as a matter of course, the Soviets fed them false

AUTHOR'S NOTE
It is extremely important to restrict the information available to the local population. This will necessitate careful screening of any locals who work near the counter-insurgency forces. Many operations have been compromised by a cleaning woman or a peasant employed to clean out the latrines.

MATCHING INTELLIGENCE TO NEEDS

information about upcoming operations. Throughout the early stages of a campaign, counter-insurgency forces will be gathering intelligence that is particularly applicable to suppressing a guerrilla movement. However, as a guerrilla war moves towards the third stage, the information required will be more akin to traditional military intelligence, with order-of-battle information becoming even more critical. Of course, if a guerrilla campaign actually progresses into the third stage of full-scale military operations, this would normally indicate that the counter-insurgency effort has had little success.

As has been illustrated again and again in successful counter-insurgency campaigns, a strong intelligence effort must be combined with a command-and-control system that recognises the importance of the intelligence and that is willing to act upon it. Although numerous cases of intelligence failures in counter-insurgencies may be cited, one of the most devastating was by the French in Indochina. Until just before their defeat, the French command refused to believe that the Viet Minh actually had the capability of winning a pitched battle against French forces. This intelligence failure not only led to the fall of Dien Bien Phu, but also to the expulsion of the French from Indochina and, arguably, because of the radicalisation of Algerian soldiers while in Viet Minh hands, following their capture during the Indochina

No matter how effective military counter-insurgency forces may be in combat against guerrilla forces, no campaign can be won without the support of a substantial portion of the population. In Malaya, Sir Gerald Templer named the operation to win over the population 'Hearts and Minds', and this has become the generic designation for attempts to gain popular support for a counter-insurgency campaign.

APPEALING TO THE POPULATION

As was discussed in the previous chapter, one function of intelligence in a counter-insurgency campaign is to identify the appeal a guerrilla force has among the population. In the case of anti-colonial uprisings, self-determination and nationalism have been tempting lures, although frequently a Marxist government is intended to replace the colonial authority. In Latin America and other parts of the world, insurgents have frequently attempted to overthrow a ruling oligarchy that is out of touch with popular aspirations. In other instances, minority-rule governments – as in Rhodesia and South Africa – have nudged large portions of the population towards an insurgency. Often, horrendous living conditions and poverty encourage the lowest classes to support an insurgency in the hope of achieving some improvement in their living standards.

CHAPTER 5

THE NEED FOR A HEARTS-AND-MINDS CAMPAIGN

To properly understand the necessity of an effective hearts-and-minds campaign to win popular support for a counter-insurgency effort, Julian Paget's list of five things that guerrillas need to pursue a successful campaign (in his book *Counterinsurgency Operations: Techniques of Guerrilla Warfare*) must be considered:

1 **A cause for which to fight.**
2 **Support from the population.**

3 **Bases.**
4 **Mobility.**
5 **Supplies.**

Without the support of the people, it is very difficult for the guerrilla to consistently attain any of these necessities, and certainly not all of them. Generally it has been the case that fewer than ten per cent of a population are true supporters of an insurgency. In most cases, the other

EXAMPLE

An interesting example of the dual effectiveness of the home guard as a method of showing confidence in the population and as a practical military tool occurred in Kenya. Despite the fact that up to ninety per cent of the Kikuyu tribe were thought to have taken some type of Mau Mau oath, a Kikuyu home guard was recruited and armed. It proved very loyal and, together with the Kikuyu Tribal Police, accounted for forty-two per cent of all Mau Mau killed during the counter-insurgency campaign.

ninety per cent are afraid of the guerrillas and may give support to ensure self-preservation. Therefore, a good hearts-and-minds campaign combined with effective psy-ops and the formation of a home guard or village defence force, which allows the people to defend themselves when government forces aren't around, will effectively 'dry up' the sea in which Mao's guerrilla fish swim.

GUERRILLA TECHNIQUES FOR WINNING OVER A POPULATION

Guerrillas will normally attempt to gain or retain the support of the population, using a variety of methods, including:

- **Attraction of a charismatic leader.** Fidel Castro and Mao Tse-tung are good examples.
- **Ideological or theological appeals.** Insurgencies based on religion – such as Islam – or Marxism-Leninism are good examples.
- **Emphasis on valid grievances.** Underemployment of an educated middle class or corrupt officials and

inequitable tax burden on the peasants are good examples.

- **Terrorism.** The insurgents demonstrate the weakness of the government and the ruling class through terror attacks on unpopular individuals or institutions.
- **Provocation.** Guerrilla movements may carry out actions designed to cause an over-reaction on the part of the government, which will alienate a substantial portion of the population.
- **Demonstration of guerrilla potency.** By providing services the government cannot offer – such as feeding or educating the peasants, or eliminating abusive landlords – while defeating government police or military forces, the guerrillas appear to be a more viable force than the government.
- **Coercion.** In some cases, the guerrillas will use fear to retain the support of the population. Huk 'terror forces' and Malayan Communist Party 'Blood and Steel Corps' units, for example, were tasked with intimidating the population and local government

officials into co-operating. Many other guerrilla movements have used coercion to a greater or lesser extent. This is one reason why establishing local self-defence forces is normally a high priority in counter-insurgency operations.

GOVERNMENT REFORM

One of the most critical steps in winning the hearts and minds of a population is government reform. Free elections can convince a population that it has a real stake in the government, although security forces will have to make sure that guerrillas do not intimidate voters.

THE CORROSIVE EFFECTS OF CORRUPTION

Eliminating corruption that channels aid into the pockets of members of the ruling party, or into a military designed more for internal security than for national defence, is also a high priority. When a peasant with very little income has to pay bribes whenever he comes into contact with the government, guerrillas trained in Mao's techniques of winning over the people become a very appealing alternative. Government apathy and inefficiency must also be overcome so that rural and poor sections of the population, which would offer fertile recruiting grounds for guerrillas, see tangible benefits from the government.

EXAMPLE

One of the first and most effective steps Magsaysay took when he came to power in the Philippines was to dismiss many corrupt and inefficient government officials and military officers. This laid the foundations for his successful counter-insurgency campaign against the Huks.

Even in most Western democracies, there is distrust of the government and an assumption of inefficient bureaucracy; in many developing countries, this attitude is far more widespread and far more justified.

CHANGE FOR THE GOOD

In some cases, a change in government must be the first step in fighting a counter-insurgency campaign. Once a government is in place that is committed to defeating a guerrilla movement both militarily and politically, a concerted attempt to win the hearts and minds of the population can be carried out through a variety of civic action programmes.

EXAMPLE

In Oman, Sultan Sa'id bin Taymur had to be deposed by his more progressive son, Qaboos bin Sa'id, before a successful hearts-and-minds campaign could be implemented. Combining psy-ops with assistance to Qaboos, the British planted rumours in newspapers before the coup that the old sultan was thinking of abdicating. Likewise, in Vietnam, the assassination of President Diem was deemed a necessary prelude to countering the Viet Cong threat.

CIVIC ACTION PROGRAMMES

According to US Special Forces manual FM31-20, Special Forces Operational Techniques, civic action environmental improvement programmes are designed to:

1 Contribute to the betterment of the lives of the local population.

2 Gain the support, loyalty and respect of the people for the government, and contribute, in some measure, to national development.

IMPORTANT CONSIDERATIONS

The US Army Special Forces, which have had extensive experience in civic action programmes developed to support counter-insurgency operations, admonish military units that become involved in such projects to keep in mind the following considerations:

1 The local population should choose the projects they deem important so that they will maintain them.

2 The population should be involved in the work so that they will feel 'ownership'.

3 Although projects should be chosen based on the desires of the locals, they should also contribute to the national development plan for the region.

4 Projects should be evaluated so that they do not seem to favour a certain segment of the population, thus becoming a propaganda victory for the guerrillas.

5 Projects should be allocated so that loyal villages receive as much attention as those of doubtful loyalty, which may be targeted for a hearts-and-minds campaign.

6 Villagers should understand the rationale behind a project (*ie* a project to ensure clean water will prevent disease).

7 Provisions should be made for maintenance of a project in the future after it is completed, which may necessitate periodic inspection or supply of materials.

8 Projects should be carried out in conjunction with international aid organisations when feasible.

VALUABLE SKILLS

Engineering personnel assigned to work with the local population on civic action construction projects should have excellent people skills, particularly the ability to work with indigenous peoples. US Special Forces engineering NCOs learn a combination of standard military engineering, including demolition and civic action construction techniques. They also learn the language of their area of likely deployment and how to teach unskilled peasants basic construction skills. Another important aspect of civic action construction projects is employing locally available materials whenever possible to make the effort relatively self-sufficient. For example, it may not be possible to bring in a crane or a helicopter to lift sections into place for a bridge, so the application of basic pulleys and tripods is an important skill.

BUILDING TIES WITH THE LOCAL POPULATION

There are many advantages in having soldiers assist with civic action projects in the areas to which they are assigned. Most importantly, the soldiers gain a sense of responsibility to the local community and build ties with the locals, which can help counter anti-government propaganda and may well develop intelligence sources. There will also be an interchange of skills between the local people and the soldiers as they learn agricultural or building techniques from each other. In a larger context, the soldiers gain skills that will be useful in their home villages when they return from their period of military service, thus expanding the effects of the civic action projects. Finally, soldiers who already possess special construction skills, possibly learned in the military, can expand them and, perhaps, even apply them to a civilian job later.

EXAMPLE

One of the more interesting uses of soldiers for civic action occurred during the Huk insurgency in the Philippines. There, army lawyers often represented local peasants against landlords, on their own time and in civilian clothing.

LOCAL DEFENCE

While assistance in agricultural projects – such as land clearance and irrigation – and construction projects – such as building bridges and digging wells – is important, civic action programmes may also offer help in constructing village defences. For those villagers who continue to live in an area subjected to heavy guerrilla activity, defences will be vitally important and will allow a local militia, armed and trained by the counter-insurgency forces, to fight off guerrilla attacks. The potential for guerrilla infiltration or attacks on villages receiving assistance makes it necessary to take preventive measures to ensure that tools or equipment do not fall into guerrilla hands. This is particularly important if explosives are being used. As a result, those involved in the civic action programme must institute security procedures. They must also be prepared to defend themselves while carrying out construction projects.

THE VALUE OF MEDICAL AID

Although engineering civic action programmes are vital, medical assistance will often make an even more lasting impression. Indeed, it can have such a marked effect upon the lives of the local population that it reaps untold good will for the government and counter-insurgency forces. It was medical aid, in fact, that finally won over the Malayan aboriginal population to the government side and removed their support from the guerrillas.

AUTHOR'S NOTE
The author still remembers a friend of his who had retired from the SAS and was planning to return to Oman to visit all of the babies he had delivered during the counter-insurgency campaign in Dhofar, babies who were then young men and women.

Initially, members of the counter-insurgency forces should work with local medical personnel on preventive measures. It is important to determine village priorities when developing health and sanitation programmes. However, a certain amount of education may be necessary as well,

Medical civic action will often win over members of an indigenous population. In this case, a Special Forces medic makes a village health call. Military medics must remain alert to possible guerrilla ambushes, however. (*US Army*)

especially where sanitation is concerned.

It is extremely important to be aware of local taboos when offering medical assistance. In many cultures, for example, male medical personnel would be precluded from examining women. When sufficient trust has developed, however, many such taboos can be overcome.

Often, a very effective technique for beginning a medical assistance programme is to have the village council or elders select some of their people for basic medical training. Such training will usually include:

- causes of disease (germs and parasites);
- basic sanitation for food and water;
- personal hygiene;
- village sanitation (latrines, bathing facilities);
- pre- and post-natal care;
- nutrition;
- control of insects and rodents.

As a village's health priorities become apparent, a large number of villagers can be engaged in general improvements, such as waste disposal, food and water inspection, and rodent control.

When implementing medical civic action programmes, the US Army Special Forces operates by eight basic rules:

1 Know the local population and leaders.

2 Avoid interference with local customs.

3 Teach people to help themselves.

4 Keep the programmes simple and practical.

5 Build momentum for programmes.

6 Build trust.

7 Make the programmes convenient and, where possible, enjoyable.

8 Plan programmes that will last.

Other medical assistance can be provided by employing military personnel and equipment. Military medics can arrange to carry out a 'sick call' once a week at villages being targeted for civic action programmes. In the case of seriously ill or injured villagers, medical evacuation can be provided by military ambulances or helicopters if not needed to deal with military combat injuries. If there is a local or regional hospital, military medical personnel can volunteer a few hours' assistance when off-duty. Surplus equipment, which is not needed by the military, may be donated or loaned to bolster village or regional medical facilities. This can include generators, old military ambulances, old stretchers, etc. Frequently, military medical units will have medicines that are approaching their 'use by' dates. If they are within a few weeks of being thrown away, they might be far better utilised if donated to local medical personnel who may well be very short of all medicines.

Another aspect of medical civic action, which can prove highly valuable in winning over peasant populations, is veterinary assistance. Often, animals are the most valuable possessions in an agrarian society, and improvements to their health will be greatly appreciated by their owners.

SOLDIERS: A VALUABLE RESOURCE

One of the greatest assets to a civic action programme are the soldiers operating in the area. Often, they will come from diverse backgrounds, which will allow them to assist local or regional government officials, farmers or technicians. For example, soldiers who were formerly police officers or who are military policemen can work with local police officers on investigative techniques, interrogation methods, the handling of prisoners

and other such skills. Personnel who have worked as fire fighters can instruct local villagers in basic fire prevention and fire fighting techniques, and perhaps supply a couple of fire extinguishers for village use. Soldiers who were stockmen can offer advice on animal husbandry, while those who were fishermen can suggest ways of increasing the catch.

A typical Western military unit deployed on counter-insurgency operations will probably include former carpenters, electricians, plumbers, bricklayers, computer technicians, mechanics and myriad other trades. Each of these soldiers can become a mentor and teacher to members of the local population. Many Western armies now have a substantial number of women assigned to support, if not combat, roles. Women soldiers can be invaluable in working with female members of the local population too.

A GIFT OF COMMUNICATION

Often, villages will be isolated, making communication a high priority. Today, the provision of a mobile phone and instructions for its use to the village headman can often create a simple link with the outside world, not to mention increasing his status and, thus, his loyalty to the counter-insurgency forces. If the guerrillas should take the phone at some point, then it becomes a source of intelligence as well, since the codes needed to intercept its calls or locate its user will be on file.

SUBTLE ADVANTAGES

Civic action offers both obvious and more subtle advantages. Those members of the security forces who are helping members of the local population lead better lives may gain their trust and, therefore, receive valuable intelligence. They may also deprive the guerrillas of recruits and support by retaining the villagers' loyalty to the government.

Civic action programmes that involve a significant number of soldiers working alongside members of the local population can also help counter the cynicism that often arises in those tasked with fighting a counter-insurgency campaign. Since the enemy is often amorphous, it is easy to take the view that all locals are guerrillas, and that it is safest to shoot first and ask questions later. Positive contacts between the counter-insurgency forces and members of the local population help give the soldiers and the population a much better sense of what they are fighting for.

EXAMPLE

Perhaps one of the best examples of the bonds that civic action can build is that between the Montagnards of Vietnam and members of the US Army Special Forces. Among the most loyal fighters against the Communists, the Montagnards were marked for destruction after the fall of South Vietnam. As a result, many former members of the Special Forces devoted the next two decades of their lives to moving as many Montagnards as possible to the USA for resettlement. Unlike many governments, they believed that loyalty was a two-way street.

Care must be taken, however, that civic action is publicised in such a manner that the counter-insurgency forces do reap the benefits of their actions. The opposite effect was achieved in Algeria, where the Special Administrative Sections were organised in 1955 to develop positive contact between Muslims and the government. Although the civic action programmes carried out by these sections were often successful and appreciated, Muslim youths still attributed the better

lifestyle to a French reaction forced by the actions of the ALN, the political arm of the insurgents, and the FLN, the military arm. In Southeast Asia, the USA sometimes also lost the beneficial effect of giving aid when shipments of US food were re-marked in Vietnamese as gifts from North Vietnam or some other Communist country. For civic action to be most successful, psy-ops units must make sure that the population attributes any improvements in lifestyle to the government.

POPULATION AND RESOURCE CONTROLS

Some of the most effective tools for security forces in a counter-insurgency campaign are population and resource controls. Such actions are designed to deprive the guerrillas of food, weapons and other useful materials, as well as to make recruitment from the population more difficult. Additionally, they can protect key lines of communication, strengthen government control over the population, isolate the guerrillas from the population as a whole and prevent the guerrillas from interfering with the day-to-day lives of the population. Often, an additional benefit is that population and resource controls will force the guerrillas to reveal themselves in an attempt to find food or contact sympathisers. Although such controls can be very effective, they must be linked with a strong psy-ops campaign to ensure support for the programme by the majority of the population.

EXAMPLE

In Cuba, Batista implemented draconian population control measures, including a halt in public transportation, curfews and communications control, which only served to alienate large segments of the population.

CHAPTER 6

A SUCCESSFUL CONTROL PROGRAMME

Among the important factors that can contribute to a successful population and resource control programme are:

- **Overt and covert surveillance of the population.** Although the idea of spying on a population may be abhorrent to those living in democratic societies, it is necessary when fighting a counter-insurgency campaign to allow identification of the guerrillas and their supporters.

This may entail suspension of certain civil rights to permit searches of persons, residences and other property.

- **Movement control.** Restricting the ability of guerrillas and their supporters to transport supplies or personnel clandestinely can prove a serious hindrance to an insurgency. Controls can include fuel rationing, checkpoints – both static and mobile, the latter to catch those attempting to avoid the former – travel passes, special licenses to transport specific goods, etc.
- **Requirement for manifests.** By requiring all aircraft, ships, boats, trucks and trains to carry manifests detailing the goods being transported, their point of origin and their destination, it is much easier to counter attempts to smuggle goods for the insurgents. Paperwork listing all personnel working aboard a ship, aircraft, train, etc, can help identify any guerrilla sympathisers.
- **Curfews.** Restricting movement during the hours of darkness makes it much harder for goods to be smuggled to guerrillas, and for

guerrilla 'militiamen' to slip out to commit acts of sabotage, etc.

Specific measures can also be implemented to control resources, including:

- establishment of limited-access areas for civilians;
- controls on weapons, radio transmitters, satellite phones, computers and cameras (NOTE: If a power such as the USA, which possesses sophisticated electronic intercept facilities, is involved, allowing the use of mobile phones, sat' phones and computers for communication can provide access to invaluable intelligence about guerrilla intentions.);
- requirement that civilians report all unexploded bombs or other explosives;
- control of raw materials, crops or livestock, which might be useful for guerrillas;
- control of propaganda distribution;
- establishment of price and monetary controls;
- establishment of food rationing and

restriction of amounts allowed for purchase at any one time (In Malaya, for example, in areas known to have guerrilla sympathies, rice was only sold already cooked, and canned goods were punctured when sold to prevent them from being supplied to guerrillas.);

- control of medical facilities and drugs, and requirement to report certain types of injury, such as gunshot wounds;
- destruction of crops, material, etc, belonging to the insurgents and confiscation of their assets.

ID CHECKS

Population screening and detention are other aspects of control. One of the first steps is normally the requirement for a national identification card, which contains a photograph of the holder, together with personal data, a fingerprint and an official stamp. It will be laminated or have some other form of protection against forging. To back this up, census data will be held by the police, and static and fixed checkpoints will be set up to verify that individuals possess the proper ID.

Cordon and search operations may also be combined with ID checks. Often, to make them more acceptable, they may be combined with other types of civic action, especially medical checks, inoculations, etc. Cordon and search operations may also be combined with certain types of psy-op (*ie* meetings to discuss recent operations against the guerrillas in an area).

Cordon and search operations will be discussed in some detail in Chapter 7.

RESETTLEMENT PROGRAMMES

One of the most drastic, but also most effective, methods of control is resettlement of substantial segments of the population, removing them from areas where they are either threatened by the guerrillas or supply the guerrillas with manpower and food. Once the resettlement has been carried out, it is much easier to establish free fire zones and to identify guerrilla sympathisers moving through an area. In Kenya, Mount Kenya, which was of sufficient importance to the Mau Mau that many oaths were taken while facing it, was declared a free fire zone.

AUTHOR'S NOTE

To give some idea of the scale of resettlement that may be necessary, during the counter-insurgency campaign against the Mau Mau in Kenya in the 1950s, approximately one million Kikuyu were moved into 720 protected villages to deny the insurgents access to crops, livestock and recruits.

CREATING THE RIGHT IMPRESSION

An important point to remember when carrying out resettlement is that the operation should not appear punitive, nor should it give the impression that people are being sent to concentration camps. Instead, those who are resettled should enjoy as good a life as they had in their previous location, if not better.

EXAMPLE

The classic example of a poorly planned resettlement programme occurred in Algeria, where thousands of Muslims died in mismanaged camps, which were, in reality, concentration camps. This forced many to join the FLN rather than allow themselves to be resettled.

For the best results, the following basic precepts should apply to resettlement operations:

- enough advance notice of the resettlement should be given so that families have time to prepare;
- free transport should be provided for families, their livestock and their possessions;
- each family should have its own designated home site at the new location;
- building materials to construct new homes should be provided at each home site or in a central location in the new village;
- a monetary relocation allowance should be given;

- food, clothing, blankets, livestock feed and medical supplies should be available until the village becomes self-sufficient;
- a plan for establishing markets and shops should be in place;
- temporary shelter should be provided until the new dwellings are finished.

AVOID VOLUNTARY RESETTLEMENT

Although the resettlement should be carried out in a sympathetic manner, it cannot normally be voluntary. In Algeria, the French tried voluntary resettlement in the Aures region to remove guerrilla support. Only 2000 of 250,000 accepted the resettlement, dooming it to failure. France's application of resource control was also poor in Indochina. In an attempt to deny the Viet Minh access to the rice producing areas of the Red River Delta, 1200 forts and blockhouses were constructed, while mobile patrols operated between them. Nevertheless, with 350,000 troops – about seventy per cent of the total available –

EXAMPLE

The Soviets practised a draconian alternative to resettlement in Afghanistan. In an attempt to deny the Mujahidin food supplies, they destroyed a good portion of the country's rural agricultural potential, eventually creating seven million refugees, who fled to the cities, or across the borders to Pakistan and Iran. So devastated was Afghanistan's agricultural base that, by 1985, virtually all food for the Mujahidin was being carried across the borders and stored in logistical bases, which then became Soviet targets. The destruction of Afghanistan's agricultural system also caused problems for the Soviet troops themselves, and for the residents of the cities that were, at least nominally, under the control of the Afghan government. They had to place a much greater reliance on food shipments from the Soviet republics, which were trucked along the vulnerable Salang Highway.

assigned to static defensive positions throughout the country, in May 1953, still only 2000 of about 7000 villages in the Delta were under French control.

DEFENDED HAMLETS

Often, when a portion of the population is resettled, it will be into what are known as 'defended hamlets'. Prior to establishing a defended hamlet programme, it is important to determine whether:

- the insurgency has progressed to the point where such measures are warranted;
- the development of a defended hamlet programme is actually within the capabilities of the counter-insurgency forces;
- the terrain favours the establishment of defended hamlets;
- the inhabitants will react favourably or unfavourably to the plan, and what methods of persuasion will be used to win over those who react unfavourably;
- the advantages of a defended hamlet programme will outweigh any disadvantages.

It cannot be stressed enough that the reaction of a population to the programme must be studied. Although more than four million Vietnamese peasants were relocated in the US Strategic Hamlet resettlement programme, it was not considered that most were being forced to leave ancestral lands, which held personal and even religious implications for them; thus the programme was doomed to failure.

If the decision is made to establish defended hamlets, there will be a trade-off between aspects that affect the lifestyle of the residents and defence. As a result, the following factors must be balanced:

- adequate water supply;
- access by means of roads, waterways, airstrips, etc;
- fertile farmland nearby;
- good tactical location to allow defence in case of attack;
- sites planned and laid out in advance;
- cleared areas for fields of fire;
- limited entry points with controlled access;

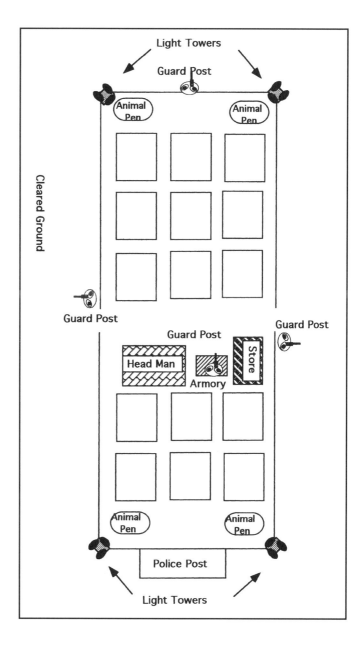

Fig. 6.1. An example of a protected village layout.

- located for mutual defence with other defended hamlets and/or so that paramilitary or military forces can quickly reinforce the hamlet.

EXAMPLE

In Algeria, the *regroupement* programme, as resettlement was termed, placed defended hamlets near military camps, then employed military civic action by having troops assigned to those camps help the villagers with improvement projects.

VARIATIONS ON A THEME

Although many defended hamlet programmes are designed to protect villagers from guerrilla influence, in the Philippines EDCOR (Economic Development Corps) moved settlers, including captured Huks, to virgin land where schools, medical care, water and protection were provided. Additionally, those relocated received help from the army in clearing land and building homes.

Perhaps the most effective resettlement programme, and the one on which many later schemes were based, was the Briggs Plan in Malaya, where 500,000 Chinese squatters were resettled away from the edge of the jungle. On the other hand, it must be understood that resettlement will not work well in all cases. Although resettlement was often successful in Malaya, it was a failure with jungle aborigines.

Protected hamlets do not always have to be agricultural outposts either. Again in Malaya, protected hamlets were established for workers in the tin mines and on rubber plantations. To provide protection for critical installations such as these, by 1949, the Malayan Special Constabulary – composed of Malays with hundreds of ex-Palestine Police NCOs – had reached a strength of 30,000.

A KEY ROLE

It should be understood that resettlement is not an end unto itself. The Briggs Plan actually had four main components:

1 To make populated areas secure.
2 To destroy the covert guerrilla organisation within populated areas.

3 To isolate the guerrillas from their sources of food and manpower.

4 To force the guerrillas to engage the security forces on ground chosen by the police or military.

The resettlement programme played a key role in achieving all four goals.

ALTERNATIVES TO RESETTLEMENT

In cases where the population is temperamentally unsuited for resettlement, creative alternatives may be tried. In Dhofar, for example, the independent nature of the local population made the establishment of defended hamlets untenable. Instead, the Omani government, with British assistance, made certain areas of the Jebel so appealing, by digging wells and providing veterinary care for cattle, that the indigenous population would congregate nearby. This programme, combined with local defence provided by the very effective *firqats*, a force formed primarily from former guerrillas and trained by the SAS, made the counter-insurgency campaign quite effective without the need for protected hamlets. When the SAS deployed to Oman after Qaboos had assumed power, they actually employed five primary elements in their counter-insurgency campaign:

1 An intelligence unit.

2 A psy-ops team.

3 A medical team including SAS medics.

4 A veterinary officer.

5 Training teams for the *firqats*.

DEALING WITH INSURGENTS

As part of the population control programme, plans must be made for detaining and interrogating insurgents, much as the USA has done at Bagram Air Base in Afghanistan and Camp X-Ray at Guantanimo Bay.

Among the considerations for detaining insurgents are:

- Establish detention and interrogation facilities.

- Ensure skilled interrogators are available who speak the language or dialect of the insurgents. Although a wide variety of techniques are used by good interrogators, one that has proved especially effective in interrogating many guerrillas of peasant background is primarily to ask questions to which the answers are known. This allows the interrogator immediately to catch out the insurgent if he lies and to convince him that lying is futile. Questions to which the interrogator does not know the answers can be worked in later in the interview.
- Develop intelligence from documents or other items captured with the insurgents. Today, this will entail having computer specialists on hand who can reconstitute items 'trashed' from a hard drive.
- Remand insurgents for trial or send them for rehabilitation when the interrogation process is complete. In some cases, they may be offered the option of co-operating with the security forces or becoming pseudo-guerrillas.
- Act on intelligence gained from

interrogations and analysis of captured materials. This can include surveillance of known haunts of captured guerrillas to identify their accomplices.

AMNESTY PROGRAMME

An effective amnesty programme will allow those guerrillas who are not especially committed, or who become disaffected, to switch to the government side. To succeed, such a programme must allow guerrillas to surrender without fear of punishment for past acts; it must be fair and well-publicised to be effective. In Malaya, for example, during 1956 alone, one hundred million leaflets were air dropped offering amnesty and rewards for turning in guerrillas. Often, word of mouth from guerrillas who have defected will help convince others to surrender. Finally, there must be a rehabilitation programme that allows former guerrillas to rejoin society. In cases where turned guerrillas have co-operated with security forces, such as the Mau Mau insurgency, it has been found that there are three critical elements in convincing a guerrilla to switch allegiances:

1 An incentive to change sides.

2 A realisation that if he does not change sides, he faces dire consequences.

3 An opportunity to prove to himself and others that what he is doing is not dishonourable.

In the case of the Mau Mau, it was also found that the administration of an anti-Mau Mau oath by a government witch doctor, to cancel out the original Mau Mau oath, was an important element of rehabilitation!

As has already been stated, but must be re-emphasised, for population and resource control measures to work, the people must be convinced that they are not punitive, but necessary. Diplomacy and fairness on the part of those representatives of the government implementing such controls are absolute necessities, as are well planned psychological operations in support of control measures.

CHAPTER 7

INDIGENOUS COUNTER-INSURGENCY FORCES

When military forces are committed to a counter-insurgency campaign, especially when those forces are deployed by a major power to assist a friendly government, such forces normally carry out six military roles:

1 **Advisory.**
2 **Tactical operations.**
3 **Civil affairs.**
4 **Intelligence.**
5 **Population and resource control.**
6 **Psychological operations.**

Roles 3–6 have already been discussed; this and subsequent chapters will concentrate on military operations against the guerrillas, and on raising and training local forces to carry out those operations. It is important to remember that during Phase 1 of an insurgency, civic action will take the pre-eminent role, but during Phases 2 and 3, offensive and defensive military operations will assume primacy. However, retaining the support of the population remains absolutely critical, so military operations must be planned to keep civilian casualties to the minimum. Unfortunately, during a counter-insurgency campaign, the term 'civilian' often becomes somewhat confusing, since guerrillas will attempt to merge with the population – as Mao termed it: 'to swim as a fish in the sea of the people'.

SELECTING ADVISORS

If advisors from a major power are assigned to work with the army of a less developed country facing an insurgency, it is important that they be chosen for their diplomatic skills and empathy with other cultures. The armed forces of different countries will reflect the cultures of those countries, and differences must be taken into consideration. Nevertheless, certain basic skills must be stressed. Experience has shown that developing an awareness of the importance of keeping information secure is critical. Otherwise, the guerrillas will know of every major operation in advance, since Captain Local will tell his cousin, who will tell his fishmonger, who will tell his mistress, who will tell her brother, who is a guerrilla. Military discipline must be stressed as well, although it is unlikely that it will reach the levels found in US and British forces. It is essential to work with junior officers and NCOs so that they develop technical proficiency and tactical skills, which they can pass on to their troops, and also to teach them the importance of teamwork and concern for the health of their troops.

COUNTER-INSURGENCY MILITARY OPERATIONS

The primary military counter-insurgency forces will conduct three major types of operation:

1 **Consolidation.** These operations are intended to restore government control over the population and areas of guerrilla operations, allowing relatively normal activities to take place.

2 **Strike.** These operations target guerrilla forces and bases in contested areas, and normally will be carried out by highly mobile special-operations, airborne or air-mobile units.

3 **Remote-area.** These operations are launched to establish strongholds in contested areas, from which counter-insurgency forces can launch attacks, set ambushes and carry out patrols against the guerrillas. As an 'in your face' challenge to guerrilla hegemony, remote-area ops may also be used to lure guerrillas into attacking. Of course, sometimes such operations result in a larger guerrilla response than expected, as at Dien Bien Phu. Some critics who do not understand the US operation at Khe Sanh have made the mistake of comparing it to Dien Bien Phu, but Khe Sanh was actually an excellent example of establishing a base that attracted massive enemy response, resulting in large-scale NVA/VC casualties.

Note that all three of these types of operation may be carried out simultaneously in one or more

During counter-insurgency campaigns, many troops must be assigned to security duties. (*USMC*)

provinces. Consolidation operations normally require a combination of military action, civic action and political action. Many counter-insurgency strategists believe that consolidation operations work best when they begin in a controlled area, then expand outward to establish government control over an ever-expanding region. In Indochina, the French termed this the 'oil slick' strategy.

THE KEYS TO SUCCESSFUL CONSOLIDATION OPERATIONS

For consolidation operations to be successful, it is necessary that the counter-insurgency forces:

- have enough military assets to defeat the guerrillas in the field;
- have enough civil affairs assets to carry out population control and civic development;

- have cleared insurgent forces from the area;
- have eliminated the most dedicated members of the guerrilla organisation (The US Phoenix Program, which was much vilified during the Vietnam War, was a good example of an operation that targeted the guerrilla infrastructure.);
- have enough security personnel to defend an area once it has been cleared of guerrillas.

Offensive operations during the consolidation phase are often effective if long-range reconnaissance patrols are used to gather intelligence and locate guerrilla forces; at which point, strike operations may be launched. In carrying out offensive operations, it is important first to locate guerrillas, and their routes into and out of an area. Once infiltration routes and guerrilla concentrations have been located, strike units can move to block escape routes by setting ambushes and positioning quick-reaction forces. When escape routes have been covered, small forces may be used to fix guerrilla units in place. Then strike forces can be committed to destroy the guerrillas, or air strikes and/or artillery support may be called in. Finally, if reserves are needed to mop up remaining guerrillas, they should be inserted.

EXAMPLE

During the Rhodesian counter-insurgency war, the Rhodesian Light Infantry made myriad parachute jumps to block the escape routes of retreating insurgents and established a reputation for eliminating large numbers of guerrillas.

SMALL-UNIT PATROLS

In addition to long-range recon patrols tasked with locating guerrilla concentrations and bases, rigorous small-unit patrols must be carried out around the clock to counter small-scale guerrilla operations. Such patrols can set up checkpoints and ambushes, but should not be tied to a schedule. They should patrol areas rather than be static, and should be very flexible. Additionally, when guerrilla operations are anticipated, area ambushes can be planned, in which numerous small

Rigorous patrolling is an important aspect of counter-insurgency warfare, and is carried out here by US Marines in Vietnam. (*USMC*)

patrols set ambushes throughout a region of guerrilla operations. Small units may also be used to raid villages known to support guerrillas.

In operations against large insurgent units, it is important to remember that guerrillas are not committed to holding ground, and will escape if not fixed and smashed with overwhelming firepower. As a result, a quick-reaction force, preferably air-mobile, must be available to rapidly saturate an area when a large guerrilla force is located.

BASIC REQUIREMENTS FOR SUCCESS

The most successful military counter-insurgency operations have normally been based on four elements:

1 Forces whose mobility matched or bettered that of the guerrillas.

2 Excellent small-unit leadership.

3 Intelligence from varied sources.

4 Special-operations forces that can stay in the field for extended periods to track the guerrillas.

These four basic requirements for the primary counter-insurgency forces should be borne in mind when considering any of the consolidation operations to be discussed.

OFFENSIVE OPERATIONS

The following general precepts for offensive operations will usually apply during the consolidation phase:

- patrol vigorously around villages, installations, etc, and employ mobile checkpoints on roads;
- set ambushes with blocking forces to cover escape routes;
- carry out raids against guerrilla bases, sympathetic villages, etc;
- remain on the offensive – defensive actions should be used to support offensive operations and maintain security in areas where offensives are not currently taking place; keep a quick-reaction reserve force;
- have security units available to escort supply convoys (see more detailed information on convoys later);
- make fire support available over as much of the operational area as possible; keep helicopter gunships or other air support on strip alert;
- hammer the insurgents hard whenever they are located; remember that injured guerrillas will not normally have access to good medical care and will lower the morale of others as they suffer;
- carry out night operations to gain surprise;
- keep up the pressure on the insurgents;
- keep up offensive operations in all types of weather.

DEFENSIVE MEASURES

Defensive operations will also be carried out during the consolidation phase. Such operations are intended to:

- deter guerrilla offensive operations: the best defence is a good offence;
- reduce the guerrillas' ability to conduct offensive operations;
- interdict guerrilla infiltration routes;
- cut off guerrilla support from inside and outside the area;
- destroy guerrilla forces whenever possible;
- lay the foundation for other counter-guerrilla activities (*ie* establish an environment that allows civic action to be implemented);
- allocate forces so that mobile reserves are available to strike at the guerrillas wherever they may appear.

Some basic defensive precepts may be established, too, for protecting critical facilities, villages or other areas:

- When establishing defensive positions, incorporate all-round protection, including physical barriers such as trenches, minefields, wire, etc.
- Incorporate bunkers within the defensive positions and lay them out for mutual support (*ie* in a zigzag pattern).
- Develop an illumination plan in the event of an attack, using spotlights and flares.
- Position guards around villages, installations, etc, to prevent infiltration. Reserves should be available to reinforce areas that come under attack.
- Provide multiple means of communication within a defensive perimeter and also to fire support, reinforcements, higher command, and so on.
- Keep movement within a perimeter to a minimum at night, so that infiltrators will be more easily spotted.
- Disperse command personnel, communications and heavy weapons so that they cannot be pre-targeted. There should be a clear chain of command in case of

losses. Contingency plans should be made for medical evacuation if communications are cut, etc.

- Ensure close supervision of civilian workers and do not allow them to stay at night. A good example of the need to supervise local civilian workers occurred at some US installations in Vietnam, where it was found that infiltrators would turn some of the Claymore mines guarding the perimeter so that they faced inwards. Had they been detonated during an attack, they would have inflicted casualties on the defenders rather than the attackers. On at least one base, this was countered by booby-trapping some Claymore mines so that they detonated if moved.
- After an attack, bear in mind that guerrillas may have booby-trapped bodies or equipment left on the battlefield.
- Try not to reveal the positioning of automatic-weapons positions until an actual attack.
- On dark nights, increase patrols and set more ambush sites. Vary patrol schedules, change passwords frequently, do not fall into a set pattern.
- If defensive positions have been established based on the location of a village or installation, rather than on desirable defensive terrain – for example, the facility or village may be overlooked by high ground – it may be necessary to establish outposts or carry out patrols to prevent the enemy from moving rocket launchers or mortars into position.
- Plan for mutual assistance from nearby villages or bases; this can include calling on reserves or pre-zeroed fire support from a central location.
- Make arrangements to secure food supplies, weapons and other equipment so that guerrilla infiltrators cannot pilfer items that may assist them.

PROTECTING ROAD CONVOYS

Defending convoys carrying food, weapons, equipment, medical supplies and other such items is very important, as they can be appealing targets for guerrillas (see *fig. 7.1*). Not

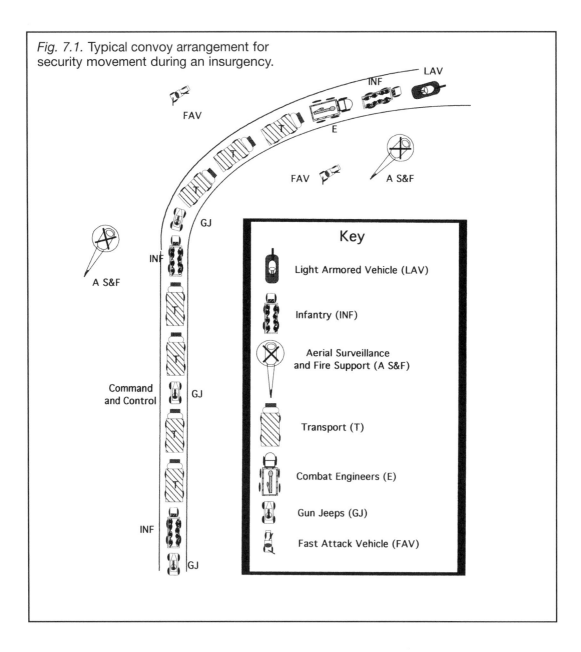

Fig. 7.1. Typical convoy arrangement for security movement during an insurgency.

Key

Light Armored Vehicle (LAV)

Infantry (INF)

Aerial Surveillance and Fire Support (A S&F)

Transport (T)

Combat Engineers (E)

Gun Jeeps (GJ)

Fast Attack Vehicle (FAV)

Convoy security is important to keep supply lines open during a counter-insurgency campaign. This French convoy was ambushed by the Viet Minh. (*ECP Army*)

only do convoys offer a source of essential supplies for guerrillas, but also they provide an opportunity to prove that the government cannot control the roads.

The following defensive measures for convoys are important:

- co-ordinate air and ground support along the route;
- develop and employ a counter-ambush SOP (standard operating procedure);
- establish security forces along the route to be taken, particularly at the most likely ambush sites;
- include security elements in the convoy. The location of command personnel, communications vehicles and heavy-weapons vehicles should vary within the convoy;
- include medical personnel, even an ambulance, in the convoy;
- make reserves available for quick support, especially air-mobile units. A strong combat reserve at the rear of the convoy allows quick reinforcement of other elements;
- spread fire support throughout the column, such as gun jeeps, APCs (armoured personnel carriers), etc;

Rhodesian counter-insurgency troops made good use of improvised armoured vehicles during their operations against guerrillas. (*David Scott-Donelan*)

- use as many diesel powered vehicles as possible, as diesel fuel is less flammable than petroleum;
- decide in advance the elements that will return fire from within vehicles during an attack to cover the infantry, who will dismount and launch a counterattack;
- make sure that vehicles carrying infantry are rigged for quick dismounting (*ie* with their tailgates well oiled, etc);
- include combat engineers for mine clearing, checking bridges, etc;

- maintain good communications throughout the column and with a command centre;
- vary speed, but clear dangerous areas as rapidly as possible. Most of all, it is important to avoid becoming caught in a killing zone. As a result, it may be necessary to push damaged vehicles off the road; however, it must be borne in mind that the sides of the road at an ambush site may be mined. If possible, include recovery vehicles in the make-up of the convoy;

EXAMPLE

The need for convoys was particularly pronounced during the Soviet campaign in Afghanistan. The Salang Highway was the primary logistical route for Soviet and Afghan government troops, with seventy-five per cent of Soviet ground traffic passing along it, while all fuel flowed through the pipeline that ran alongside the road. As a result, the highway and the Salang Tunnel, through which it passed, were prime targets for the Mujahidin, and the Soviets had to devote substantial assets to defending them. The latter achieved some success in protecting convoys and mounted troops by using a leapfrogging 'over-watch' approach. This tactic entailed moving combat vehicles on to heights that overlooked a route while a convoy or mounted unit passed. The scheme was also employed successfully using air-mobile troops, who would be lifted into over-watch positions.

- check with members of the local population for any suspicious activity along the road.

In Indochina, the French found themselves in the situation where convoys supplying outposts often had to fight their way along a 'highway of death', where guerrilla ambushes were a matter of course. Counter-insurgency forces must avoid allowing the guerrillas to control roads. Any attack on a convoy must be far more costly to the guerrillas than to the security forces.

PROTECTING RAILWAYS

In many countries, railways are the primary mode of transport for goods; thus, it is necessary to plan for security aboard trains, since guerrillas will know the route a train must take and, in many cases, its schedule. Varying schedules can make it more difficult for guerrillas to strike, as can patrolling the tracks. Guards at bridges, rail yards and stations can help prevent sabotage.

In areas where there is a strong threat of guerrilla attack, armoured trains may be used to patrol the tracks or to clear them ahead of trains carrying high-priority goods. Generally, however, regular freight trains can be used with a few alterations. Open wagons can have sandbags added and act as carriers for mortars, machine-guns or other heavy weapons. These wagons should not be placed next to those carrying fuel or explosives. Locomotives will normally be preceded by a pair of flatbed wagons carrying sandbags, rocks, scrap steel or other heavy materials to set off any mines and cushion impact against obstructions. Decoy trains, which appear to be unarmed passenger or freight trains, but that actually carry troops and heavy weapons in disguised wagons, have been quite effective in drawing guerrilla attacks. In most cases, however, guerrillas will find it easier to derail trains rather than attack them; thus, patrolling the tracks is extremely important. As with most counter-insurgency operations, good communications are necessary among troops on a train and with military bases along the line.

On single-track railways in areas where guerrilla attacks might occur, the US Army manual Counterguerrilla Operations, FM31-16 recommends using the 'positive block' system of operations. When employing this system, the line is divided into blocks, and a train cannot enter a block until any preceding train has cleared it. This allows a train that runs into an ambush to reverse along the track to escape, and also permits a train carrying reinforcements to approach from either direction.

CORDON AND SEARCH OPERATIONS

Limiting guerrilla support among the local population will generally require cordon and search operations to be carried out around villages suspected of aiding the enemy. In such operations, it is necessary to descend upon the area quickly and with surprise. A prior rehearsal on a mock village at a training facility will allow the operation to proceed more smoothly.

A cordon should be established

Cordon and search operations are an important technique for denying guerrillas support. (*USMC*)

immediately to prevent anyone from leaving the area. This cordon should include checkpoints and road-blocks to control entry and exit. The blocking force must have sufficient strength that it can fight off attackers from outside the village attempting to get in. The actual search force should divide the area into zones, with a search unit assigned to each zone. The search parties are normally split into a search element, a security element and a reserve element. Whenever possible, some personnel who are native to the area, or who have served there long enough to be familiar with the village, should be included. Guerrilla weapons, papers or other material found may be highly desirable from an intelligence point of view, but care must be taken to check that they are not booby-trapped. Although the initial descent upon the village should be quick, it is important to allow enough time to carry out a thorough search and interrogations.

As an example of the potential success achievable by cordon and search operations, in Palestine during the Jewish insurgency prior to independence, British forces carried out 170 cordon and search operations,

EXAMPLE

Probably the most successful cordon and search operation was Operation Anvil, carried out against the Mau Mau. Since the Kikuyu Reserve bordered Nairobi, there was a strong core of support for the guerrillas there, and many Mau Mau leaders used Nairobi as a base. Anvil was a massive operation that covered the entire city. As many as 20,000 suspected Mau Mau were detained, and IDs were issued to those residents who were cleared, making it easy to identify any Mau Mau entering the city in the future. Anvil succeeded in separating the Mau Mau from their primary source of supply and, in ridding the city of the insurgents, also lowered its crime rate substantially. Later, surprise sweeps were carried out in Nairobi to snare any Mau Mau still there, but Anvil had taken the heart out of the insurgency.

Counter-insurgency sweeps in the tribal lands and forests by the King's African Rifles (KAR), a highly decorated African unit with European officers, were also quite successful. Interestingly, the Kikuyu were traditionally better educated and urbanised than other tribes and, as a result, rarely joined the KAR, thus helping to ensure its loyalty.

Among the most effective counter-guerrilla operations were 'Population Sweeps', which allowed a substantial section of the loyal African population to take part in operations against the Mau Mau. In these sweeps, up to 70,000 Africans, men and women, would line up shoulder to shoulder with their *pangas* (a form of machete) and begin hacking away at the forest. Members of the Kenya Police backed them up, but many Mau Mau were hacked to pieces by this primitive 'neighbourhood watch' programme.

of which about seventy-five per cent led to the discovery of at least some weapons, illegal immigrants or other 'contraband'. On the other hand, many searches were followed by complaints alleging looting or brutality by British forces. Ironically, recent Israeli cordon and search operations in Palestinian areas have elicited the same complaints. Every attempt must be made to avoid giving grounds for such complaints, and troops must be closely supervised by their officers.

BLOCK AND SWEEP

The Soviet Army employed its own version of the cordon and search operation in Afghanistan, which it described as 'block and sweep'. The three basic precepts for a block and sweep operation were:

1 Use recon troops to find the location of guerrillas.

2 Pin down the guerrillas while air assault and other blocking troops move into position to prevent them from escaping or manoeuvring.

3 Destroy the guerrilla units using the sweeping forces.

SEARCH OUT SUBTERRANEAN HIDES

Guerrillas have traditionally hidden themselves or their supplies underground or even under water, so a great effort must be made to search for such subterranean hides. Dogs are very useful in carrying out these searches, as are mine detectors and other forms of metal detector. Some

Since guerrillas often use underground storage areas for their supplies, specialist troops, such as these 'tunnel rats', may be needed. (*US Army*)

EXAMPLE

In Vietnam, Viet Cong underground complexes often contained barracks, hospitals, armouries and extensive warrens of rooms and tunnels. Generally, the tunnel complexes were designed with escape routes and were booby-trapped. Although US troops used CS gas at times when attempting to clear the tunnels, the most effective device proved to be the 'Mark 1 Infantryman, Size Small'. Generally, small, tough and wiry infantrymen were specially selected for their ability to operate in tunnels. Known as 'tunnel rats', they frequently carried only a handgun, torch and fighting knife.

---

guerrilla units have constructed underground tunnel complexes that have required highly specialised search skills to discover them.

Although offensive and defensive

IRREGULAR FORCES

actions by regular military units – either of the country facing the insurgency or of an allied nation – are important, operations carried out by locally recruited irregulars will be of equal significance in a counter-insurgency campaign. The US Army Special Forces, and the British and Australian Special Air Services have been very successful in raising local irregular forces to assist in counter-insurgency campaigns. In fact, it was the successes of the SAS in Malaya that led to its re-activation as a regular military unit. In many cases, such local forces will have differing degrees of training and varying missions.

The US Special Forces often break irregular forces into three basic groups:

Civil Guard Units. These forces have
1 the mission of assisting with internal security. Their training includes the use of weapons ranging from small arms to heavy machine-guns and mortars; basic communications so that they can call in assistance; the carrying out

of raids and ambushes; and the pursuit of guerrilla forces. Often, Civil Guard Units will be trained to assist regular special-operations forces.

Village Defence Forces. The main **2** function of these forces is to protect their individual villages and nearby facilities, such as schools, bridges, agricultural storehouses, etc. Village Defence Forces are not full-time units and normally will have training in the use of small arms up to medium

machine-guns only. A good example would be the *harkis* formed by the French in Algeria. In Malaya, where the MCP used its 'Blood and Steel Corps' to commit robberies, assassinations and intimidation of the population, eventually 250,000 Home Guardsmen were recruited to give villages the confidence to resist the guerrillas.

Civil Defence Groups. These units **3** are often recruited from primitive tribes, who are at home in the

Training local quick-reaction forces in airborne or air-mobile operations will often increase their esprit de corps and effectiveness. In this case, a member of the US Army Special Forces trains a MIKE Force member in Vietnam. (*US Army*)

roughest parts of the country facing the insurgency. Mountain peoples traditionally make especially good irregulars. Many Civil Defence forces are trained to operate along remote borders. In most cases, small groups of special forces advisors will work with CDGs, usually living among them and earning their loyalty. These forces frequently operate, in effect, as full-time paid irregulars – some use the term 'mercenaries', since it is common for them to have only minimal loyalty to a central government. They will be instructed in such skills as:

- hunter-killer techniques;
- trail watching;
- border surveillance;
- ambushes and booby-traps along guerrilla infiltration and supply routes;
- raids on guerrilla camps;
- intelligence gathering in guerrilla controlled areas.

BORDER OPERATIONS

Some of the same people who are recruited for Civil Defence Groups may be employed specifically for border surveillance, either because their villages are located near the border or because they have been moved to that area specifically to carry out the task. In addition to border surveillance, with training and special forces assistance, such 'indigs' can also carry out border denial operations. Their tactics usually include:

- rigorous patrolling along the border;
- small squad-sized operations;
- surveillance from hides during the daytime, then operations against enemy targets of opportunity at night;
- clandestine operations dressed as civilians, or wearing the same attire as the guerrillas;
- penetrating enemy forces with pseudo-guerrillas (This tactic will be discussed in greater detail in Chapter 10.);
- inserting homing devices into enemy equipment found in caches to allow infiltrating guerrilla units to be tracked;
- booby-trapping enemy supplies (NOTE: In Vietnam, Operation Eldest Son planted grenades with instantaneous fuses and

ammunition with overloads, both designed to explode in the hands of the guerrillas using them. Not only did this kill and maim insurgents, but also it encouraged distrust of their weapons. The same technique was used by Force X against the Huks in the Philippines.);

- gathering intelligence on enemy movements, supply drops, bases, and so on;
- capturing enemy couriers as intelligence sources.

This use of a friendly population as a buffer along a border is an alternative to creating a restricted border zone, cleared of vegetation, where anyone entering the zone is considered to be a guerrilla and likely to be fired upon. Such 'free fire' sterile zones often are supplemented by electronic sensors, minefields, listening posts, aerial surveillance and patrols. It is possible to combine a restricted border zone with friendly elements of the population settled just inside the border.

When neighbouring countries are neutral or friendly towards the government facing an insurgency,

liaison with those countries can be very useful in border denial. Sometimes, indigenous tribes along a border will have members on both sides of it. If those tribesmen are enlisted as border watchers, they can be excellent intelligence sources.

DISGUISED SPECIAL-OPS TROOPS

In Afghanistan, the Soviets developed a relatively successful alternative to indigenous border watchers. They formed special 'caravan hunters' of Spetsnaz disguised as Mujahidin, who operated along the borders, raiding caravans that were smuggling arms and supplies. Initially, the Soviets had employed a large number of troops from their Central Asian Republics in Afghanistan, in the belief that, as Muslims, they would be more effective in dealing with the Afghans. However, since they were related ethnically to those portions of the Afghan population who were traditional foes of the Pashtuns, they were hated even more by the Mujahidin. Spetsnaz personnel drawn from Central Asia were useful for such pseudo-guerrilla units as the caravan hunters. Soviet forces also enjoyed some degree of success with ground sensors seeded along mountain trails to locate Mujahidin supply caravans, which then were subjected to air strikes.

When planning border security,

SECURING COASTLINES AND AIRPORTS

coastlines must not be neglected, and patrols must be carried out along the shoreline and at sea. Employees at ports should be vetted to ensure that they do not have guerrilla sympathies. Ships should be checked to make sure that they are not smuggling arms or guerrillas; ships' crews should be screened as well. Fishing boats have often been used to support an insurgency, so patrol craft should randomly stop and search fishing boats and other small commercial craft.

Precautions must also be taken at airports to screen ground employees and crews, and to watch for smuggling. Photographs of known

EXAMPLE
In Malaya, the jungle aborigines were not resettled and, therefore, became easy prey for the Malaysian Communist Party (MCP) when it had to retreat into the jungle. Eventually, however, members of the SAS and other military personnel helped the aborigines to form a regiment for self-defence and to fight in the jungle. In the later stages of the Malayan counter-insurgency campaign, this aboriginal unit hunted the MCP along the border with Thailand.

guerrilla sympathisers should be available to airport and port security personnel. In addition, it is advisable at airports to take precautions that will make difficult the launching of SAMs (surface-to-air missiles) against aircraft in the process of taking off or landing.

INLAND WATERWAYS
On inland waterways, checkpoints at locks, dams and bridges can help deter the smuggling of guerrillas, arms and supplies. Vegetation should be

removed from the banks at likely ambush points to protect legitimate riverine traffic and patrol forces. Defended hamlets along the waterways can place friendly sections of the population in position to counter guerrilla movements and provide intelligence.

Aerial surveillance along inland waterways can also help deter smuggling. Such aircraft should have the capability to drop flares for illumination at night. When moving weapons or other supplies useful to the guerrillas, riverine convoys can be used for mutual defence.

Yet another type of indigenous force

DEEP-PENETRATION MISSIONS

that can be highly effective in counter-insurgency warfare is one trained specifically for deep-penetration missions into guerrilla controlled areas.

A member of the US Army Special Forces trains for survival on deep-penetration patrols.

A member of the New Zealand SAS on a deep-penetration patrol during the Vietnam War. (*NZ SAS*)

Normally, a small number of special forces personnel will operate with these units as advisors and also to call in artillery support, air cover or medevac missions if needed. Indigenous recon teams assigned to MACV/SOG (Military Assistance Command Vietnam/Special Operations

Group) operated in this manner.

Among the missions allocated to indigenous special-ops teams are:

- destruction of enemy supply depots or interdiction of supply lines;
- snatching of enemy personnel or

equipment for intelligence purposes (During the Vietnam War, for example, certain pieces of equipment, such as the Dragunov sniper rifle, carried a large bounty if recovered.);

- demoralising guerrillas and creating confusion in their 'safe areas';
- keeping guerrillas moving by harrying them;
- fragmenting insurgent groups

EXAMPLE

The French made particularly good use of indigenous recon and raiding troops in Indochina, training *maquis* drawn from mountain tribes in the north of the country to act as 'guerrillas' against the Viet Minh. These units would evolve into the Groupes des Commandos Mixte Aeroportes (GCMA), which proved very effective against the Viet Minh. In fact, rumours persisted in the special-operations community for years that small GCMA units continued to operate against the Viet Minh long after the French had pulled out of Indochina.

through ambushes and other attacks;
- attacking guerrillas threatening friendly villages;
- denying guerrillas population support.

In the majority of the counter-

INVOLVEMENT OF MAJOR POWERS

insurgency campaigns fought since World War II, at least some assistance to the armed forces of the country in which the insurgency took place came from a major power. In some cases, this was the former or current colonial ruler of the country, as with the British in Kenya and Malaya. In others, assistance was given by a major power with political ties to the country facing the insurgency, such as the USA in Vietnam, the Soviets in Afghanistan and the British in Oman. Economic interests have also encouraged major powers to become involved in counter-insurgency campaigns.

Generally, the most successful counter-insurgency campaigns

US support for these Contra guerrillas in Nicaragua helped them to remove the Communist Sandanista government.

involving major powers have been those in which only a limited number of highly trained professional troops have been sent in to act as advisors or trainers, or to carry out special operations. The US Special Forces, British SAS and other such units have normally functioned well with local troops, especially indigenous irregulars drawn from minorities or dispossessed groups within a country. Not only do these special forces personnel have the skills to instruct indigenous people and carry out local civic action, but

also they are trained and conditioned to spend long periods in the bush, often in guerrilla controlled areas.

On the other hand, when large numbers of conscript troops, who have been trained for conventional warfare, are committed, as was the case of the US forces in Vietnam and Soviets in Afghanistan, the counter-insurgency campaign is usually doomed to failure. Even if a major power could win a counter-insurgency campaign with little help from local forces and by a massive commitment of personnel, its troops would have to remain as an occupying army.

Counter-insurgency operations have a

THE WILL OF THE PEOPLE

strong chance of success if the insurgency does not represent the will of the majority of the people, and a substantial portion of the population can be mobilised against the guerrillas. If the insurgency is being waged as a popular nationalistic war of liberation from an occupying power, however, recruiting the bulk of the population to act militarily or politically against the guerrillas will be very difficult. As the sentiment was often expressed by US conscript troops in

Vietnam, especially later in the war, 'If the Vietnamese are not willing to fight for their own freedom, what are we doing here?' On the other hand, the Greeks have traditionally had a strong sense of patriotism and nationalism, which was mobilised against the KKE, an organisation that most Greeks viewed as a movement supported by Albanians, Yugoslavs and Greeks outside the country.

Populations who are willing to fight against an insurgency should be given as much assistance as possible to allow them to succeed. Highly trained special forces personnel are generally the most cost effective, force multiplying method of offering that assistance.

CHAPTER 8

SMALL-UNIT OPERATIONS

Good patrolling skills are extremely important in counter-insurgency operations. Because it is so important to locate insurgents and gather intelligence about their intent, effective patrolling will play a major role in the success of a counter-insurgency campaign. Not only that, but active patrolling helps keep the initiative with the counter-insurgency forces, rather than with the guerrillas.

According to the US Army manual Advisor Handbook for Stability Operations, FM31-73, among the uses of patrols in counter-insurgency operations are:

1 Saturating an area where insurgents are suspected to be active.

2 Controlling important roads and trails.

3 Maintaining contact between villages and military units.

4 Establishing population checkpoints.

5 Providing security for friendly forces.

6 Interdicting insurgent supply routes and communications.

7 Establishing ambushes.

8 Pursuing, maintaining contact with, and destroying insurgents.

9 Providing internal security in rural areas.

10 Locating insurgent units and their base camps.

FAST-MOVING UNITS

Often, saturation patrols will be used, employing small, fast-moving units to harass and uncover insurgents. Against the Huks in the Philippines, patrols of fifteen or twenty men, who carried a lot of firepower, but could still move quickly, proved particularly effective. Such patrols will allow personnel to gain an excellent knowledge of the area of operations, to give the local population a sense of security, to gather intelligence about insurgents and to build confidence in the ability of counter-insurgency forces to keep the guerrillas on the run. One of the adjustments the Soviets had to make in Afghanistan was to give much more autonomy to junior officers leading patrols so that they could react quickly to the situation on the ground. Since the Soviet command structure did not normally encourage

individual initiative, it took a substantial change in mind set to allow junior airborne and air-assault officers this greater freedom of action.

Rhodesian troops used trucks to allow rapid follow-up of terrorist contacts. (*David Scott-Donelan*)

FAN PATROLS

In Malaya, the British found that establishing a patrol base from which small teams could fan out worked very well. In fact, one of the types of patrol widely employed was known as the 'fan' patrol. Using this system, teams comprising three or four men move out on fixed compass/GPS bearings from the base, much as the ribs of a fan project from its centre. It was discovered that the patrol lines were best located about ten degrees apart.

Four-man patrols are often used on counter-insurgency operations; in this case in Rhodesia. (*David Scott-Donelan*)

In thick jungle, teams would travel about 1000 yards, but in more open terrain, they could go farther. However, time was a greater limiting factor, as it was found that for the teams to retain their sharpness, three hours was about the maximum they could spend on patrol.

Once a team had reached its stop point, it would move a few degrees to the left or right, then return to the patrol base. The patrol commander remained at the base with a reaction force in case any teams needed reinforcement. He also maintained communications with his company commander in case a large guerrilla force was encountered.

As an alternative to the fan method, forces in Malaya would also employ the 'stream' patrol, whereby a three- or four-man team would move along one bank of a stream, then return along the other, looking for indications of a guerrilla presence near the water source.

Using these and other patrol methods, if a team spotted a guerrilla concentration, normally two men would remain to keep the guerrillas under observation and to gather intelligence, while the remainder would return to the patrol base to bring back reinforcements. Then it would be decided whether to set an ambush or call in an even greater force.

PREPARING FOR A PATROL

It is important to make careful preparations prior to a patrol. These should include studying maps and aerial reconnaissance photographs of the area to determine key landmarks and the best patrol routes. Applying a grid reference system to the area will allow efficient communications between patrols and with base. Adherence to the grid system will also reduce the likelihood of two patrols becoming engaged in a fire fight with each other. If it is necessary for a patrol to cross into part of the grid assigned to another patrol, then it is absolutely essential to communicate with that patrol. Emergency helicopter extraction zones should be determined in advance, as should rallying points in case the patrol has to take evasive action or carry out counter-ambush drills to break off contact.

It may also be a good idea to prepare patrol maps for night operations, using luminous ink and plastic covers. Do not, however, carry marked maps or other papers that can provide the guerrillas with useful intelligence. Compasses and GPS (Global Positioning System) units should be set before setting out on the patrol; the latter may be programmed with key terrain features. As with

maps, however, careful consideration must be given to the information programmed into a GPS unit in case it falls into enemy hands, as has happened occasionally in Afghanistan.

Generally, the approach should be via stream lines, ridge lines or other rough terrain. Do not approach the objective head-on, and do not walk along the tops of ridge lines so that patrol members are silhouetted.

CONCEALMENT PROCEDURES

Normal procedure includes planning steps to hide the passage of the patrol. These can include such

AUTHOR'S NOTE

During the Vietnam War, experimental jungle boots were produced for MACV/SOG, which had copies of bare Vietnamese-size feet moulded into the soles. Intended to leave footprints that appeared to be those of local peasants, these boots never really made it past the testing stage, at least partially because the heavier Americans left deeper impressions than would the Vietnamese.

measures as having the last man run a branch over footprints to remove them, and making sure that all patrol members are careful not to let branches rub against each other or cause leaves to rustle. Some recon patrol members may choose to wear non-military footwear so that any

An SAS patrol receives a briefing prior to operations in the jungle.

footprints do not immediately indicate that soldiers have passed by.

PREPARATION OF PATROL MEMBERS

All members of the patrol should be thoroughly briefed about their mission. Prior to beginning the patrol, personnel should check their weapons and equipment for proper functioning,

and should tape all exposed metal parts, then do a 'jump test' to check for noise. Steel helmets tend to be noisy and often are left behind for patrolling. Although modern Kevlar helmets are somewhat less noisy, many still prefer 'softer' headgear, especially when carrying out clandestine recon patrols. Personnel should travel as lightly as possible, commensurate with the duration of the patrol, but must carry water bottles, binoculars, night-vision equipment, knives, wire cutters, dry socks, medical kits and other essential items. For a long patrol, arrangements will have to be made for re-supply missions. Often, when aircraft commonly over-fly a patrol area, re-supply can be carried out surreptitiously. In the early stages of the War Against Terrorism in Afghanistan, for example, the various humanitarian drops of food to the Afghans may well have had re-supply drops for special-ops personnel 'piggybacked' on to them.

If available, scout dogs are invaluable when searching for the enemy and for alerting the patrol to ambushes. For positioning and identification at night, 'Ranger eyes' or other luminous tape should be used. Apply camouflage cream to exposed body parts. Make sure that all personnel know the simple hand signals that will be used for silent communication.

CARRY OUT A REHEARSAL

Whenever possible, and provided similar terrain can be found, a rehearsal of the mission will prove invaluable. It will allow personnel to ensure that their night-vision equipment is working properly and help them adjust to using it.

A patrol rehearsal should include such basics as:

- techniques for changing formation;
- methods for crossing obstacles;
- immediate action drills;
- actions to be taken at an objective;
- hand signals;
- drills for security when stopped;
- evacuation of casualties;
- prisoner escort methods if a 'snatch' patrol is being carried out.

When carrying out the actual patrol, it is advisable to follow these basic

BASIC PATROL PROCEDURES

procedures:

- Periodically, check that all members of the patrol are accounted for.
- In addition to the passwords necessary to clear checkpoints or to return through government lines, a specific password should be chosen for members of the patrol so that they can identify themselves to other members at night.
- Normally, odd-numbered patrol members should check to the left and even-numbered members should check to the right. Additionally, there will be at least one member assigned to take the lead, and another to act as the 'tail gunner' and watch the rear.
- Move with weapons unslung and ready for action, but with the safety catches on to avoid accidents.
- Before crossing streams, roads,

trails or any other places where patrol members will be exposed, the area should be reconnoitred and security should be posted.
- Patrol members should not bunch, which would provide an inviting target for grenades, mortars, machine-guns, etc.
- When it is necessary to give orders or pass information, make sure that each patrol member receives it.
- Follow proper noise discipline.
- Have a lead/recon element slightly ahead of the bulk of the patrol, but keep a covering force near enough to respond if the lead element runs into the enemy.
- Don't leave litter, faeces or other signs that the patrol has passed.
- If the patrol stops for sleep, organise a rotation so that some members remain awake and on guard while others sleep.
- Watch for potential booby-traps and ambush sites. (*ie* an area where undergrowth or branches appear to have been pulled back and tied could indicate either).
- When checking villages, be wary of empty huts, which may have been

A counter-insurgency patrol in Rhodesia. (*David Scott-Donelan*)

booby-trapped. Also watch children for indications of potential trouble (in Vietnam, for example, at least one patrol was saved from a booby-trap when children were noticed placing their hands over their ears, as if expecting an explosion, as the patrol approached).

- Remain in contact with patrols nearby for mutual support.

- Whenever possible, stay off trails and move through underbrush or foliage. Not only will this make it less likely that booby-traps will be encountered, but also it will make the patrol harder to track.
- Take care of small injuries

immediately so that they do not become infected.

- Do not retrace the same route when returning from the patrol.

For much of the time, patrols on counter-insurgency operations will be

FIRE SUPPORT

within range of artillery fire support, as well as air support.

Fire support can have many applications, including:

- to support a raid on a guerrilla village, camp, etc;
- to destroy targets of opportunity identified by the patrol;
- to neutralise a suspected ambush site in a 'recon by fire';
- to destroy enemy personnel;
- to fix a guerrilla force and prevent it from withdrawing;
- to 'sanitise' an area around a guerrilla force to prevent reinforcements from joining it;
- to provide illumination with flares;
- to destroy material (*ie* a guerrilla

tunnel complex filled with supplies);
- to prevent guerrillas from crossing a certain point;
- to lay down smoke to cover an advance or retreat by the patrol.

Many of these fire missions fall under the old infantry officer's precept: 'Never send a man where you can send a bullet!'

Since guerrillas often use darkness to shield their movements or actions, it

NIGHT OPERATIONS

is very important that counter-insurgency forces be highly trained in carrying out night operations. Night fighting skills can be as simple as being aware of the level of moonlight and the resulting silhouettes or shadows. Those skilled at night patrolling also learn to protect their night vision. If, for example, a flare is dropped, they will keep one eye closed so that night vision is not lost completely.
Among other skills that must be mastered to operate effectively at

night are:

- firing techniques, including the establishment of fields of fire, movement after firing to hamper return fire and spotting targets;
- use of individual weapons in darkness and employment of artificial illumination, including infra-red, laser and other specialised night sighting devices;
- tactics for relieving units or installations;
- reconnaissance patrolling and security when halted;
- land navigation, including employment of GPS;
- noise and light discipline;
- offensive and defensive use of various types of electronic detection device;
- use of artillery support;
- air-mobile operations;
- airborne operations, including the use of pathfinders and Air Force Combat Control Teams;
- aerial re-supply;
- use of sensors aboard aircraft and airborne fire support, including employment of helicopter and fixed-

wing gunships.

Whether as a member of a long-range patrol or acting separately, the sniper can be employed very effectively in

EMPLOYMENT OF SNIPERS

counter-insurgency operations. Normally operating in two-man scout/sniper teams, snipers may function as an advance guard infiltrated ahead of the patrol, as a flank guard or as a rear guard assigned with counter-sniper or counter-tracker missions. Snipers who have moved into hides in advance can also provide cover for air assaults, river crossings or other operations.

On special operations, snipers can support raids or ambushes, while multiple sniper teams can move into a guerrilla infested area to set area ambushes. Snipers have also been used to initiate what is known as a 'demolition ambush'. In this case, explosives, often Claymore mines, are placed along a trail likely to be traversed by guerrilla forces. When the devices are set up, an 'electric gate' is established, which is closed by the bullet from a hidden sniper hundreds of yards away. In many cases, snipers employ the 'stay behind' technique, used to such good effect by the SAS in Northern Ireland. Originally part of a patrol that may have been spotted, at some point the sniper or snipers will go into hiding to await a juicy target.

If a patrol is compromised and encounters a superior guerrilla force, a couple of snipers can be very effective at discouraging pursuit while the rest of the patrol escapes. Snipers may also be used to destroy guerrilla equipment from long range. Since most insurgents have trouble with re-supply, damaging vehicles or other equipment can severely inhibit their operations. Another use of snipers in counter-guerrilla patrols is to carry out a 'recon by fire' when a guerrilla ambush or sniper is thought to occupy a certain location. By placing a few rounds into likely hiding places, the sniper may be able to flush, injure or kill any enemy lying in wait. During cordon and search operations, the scout/sniper team can be invaluable in covering possible escape routes from a village.

In fact, one of the greatest advantages of the sniper in counter-insurgency operations is that he may be used very surgically against the guerrillas without harming innocent civilians nearby. If, for example, guerrilla 'tax collectors' are known to extort money along a certain road, snipers can cover likely places where the tax collectors will stop traffic. The elimination of guerrillas who prey on the population with precise shots produces an excellent psychological effect, both on the guerrillas – who will have trouble finding willing volunteers to collect taxes – and among the population, who will have seen a hated parasite eliminated. The sniper can also take out guerrilla leaders, scouts, mortar men and other important personnel from a distance.

AMBUSHES AND BOOBY-TRAPS

The setting of ambushes and booby-traps has been a basic guerrilla tactic in virtually every insurgency. They allow the guerrillas to inflict casualties on government security forces, using hit-and-run tactics in the former case and simple devices in the latter. In both instances, the guerrillas will generally sustain minimal casualties. These same tactics, however, may be used very successfully against the guerrillas by small, deep-penetration counter-insurgency units. As a result, the counter-insurgency soldier must be very familiar with the techniques of ambush and with counter-ambush SOPs (Standard Operating Procedures), as well as the methods for spotting booby-traps, disarming them and constructing them.

ANATOMY OF AN AMBUSH

In simple terms, an ambush is a surprise attack launched from a concealed position. Normally, the enemy sets the time, as the ambush will conform to his schedule, but the attacker sets the place. The ambush forces will comprise an assault element, which conducts an attack against the primary enemy unit, and a security element, which isolates the ambush site and covers the withdrawal of the assault element. A well prepared ambush will take into consideration the strength and composition of the enemy forces, and the enemy's reinforcement capability. Terrain should be chosen that funnels the enemy into a killing zone, which can be covered completely by fire.

CHAPTER 9

NIGHT AMBUSHES

Night ambushes offer the advantage of more disorientation on the part of the enemy, as well as making retreat or reinforcement more difficult. On the negative side, firing positions of the ambush team will be revealed through muzzle flashes, and control of the ambush will be more difficult. Also, night ambushes will normally be broken off more quickly. If a force does plan a night ambush, care must be taken that any night-vision optics or night telescopic sights are working properly and can cover the killing zone effectively. While the day ambush is easier to control and offensive action can last longer, it will be more difficult for the ambush element to break away, especially if reinforcements arrive.

BASIC REQUIREMENTS
A well set ambush will normally conform to certain criteria:

- **All escape routes should be covered.** It is important to know the approach route the enemy will take, as well as possible alternative routes. Then, each possible escape route must be covered by assault units or booby-traps. Often, an ambush will be set with one escape route apparently left open, but in fact it will be covered by Claymore mines, detonating cord or other explosive devices. This allows additional casualties to be inflicted as the enemy attempts to escape.

- **The ambush should be sited in depth.** Not only should there be sufficient firepower at the ambush site to prevent escape, but also a stop group should be placed along the approach route to cut off any retreat, while secondary ambushes may be set along possible escape routes. Explosive ambushes may be set as well, as discussed above. Designated personnel should be assigned to engage advance and rear guards so that they cannot reinforce the main element when it comes under attack.

- **Good fields of fire should be ensured from all positions.** The personnel setting the ambush should know the capabilities of their weapons and their own capabilities, as well as the proper tactical use of the weapons during an ambush. They must maintain fire discipline until the ambush is triggered, and should have pre-arranged fields of fire to ensure that they do not endanger other members of their unit and also engage all members of the enemy force. Arcs of fire are important to prevent members of the ambush team from being caught in their own crossfire. One technique is to place sticks or other unobtrusive markers to delineate safe arcs of fire. If the ambush is part of a 'snatch' operation to gain a prisoner for interrogation, everyone should be aware of who not to shoot.

- **Strict discipline must be maintained.** In addition to maintaining fire discipline, those setting the ambush must maintain communications discipline and must adhere to the plan. If the unit commander, a sniper or some other member of the ambush team is slated to initiate the ambush, fire should be held until he fires, unless some unforeseen circumstance arises that requires instant engagement. Once the ambush has been launched, it should be carried out ruthlessly, eliminating every enemy in the killing zone if possible. If all of the enemy are killed and a search is to be made for intelligence, it should be carried out carefully by a two-man team, one man covering the other in case any

of the guerrillas are 'playing possum'.

- **Planning must be detailed and every team member must be thoroughly briefed.** The ambush area should have been well reconnoitred and all available intelligence about enemy movements considered when siting it. The plan should factor in contingencies for calling off the ambush or for disengagement if anything goes wrong. Personnel should be well briefed, and rehearsals should be carried out on the site if possible. This may not always be the case when operating in enemy territory, so standard ambush procedures should be practised before launching the mission.

- **Security should be maintained.** Care should be taken that no tell-tale signs of the presence of the ambush party are left near the ambush site. Noise discipline and communications security must be maintained near the site as well. Personnel setting the ambush should be experienced enough to remain quietly in place long enough for the enemy to enter the killing zone. Sentries must be posted too, to cover the backs of those setting the ambush so that they are not ambushed themselves. A password should be chosen for use by members of all elements of the ambush team.

- **The ambush should be carefully laid and sited.** Whenever possible, natural obstacles, such as rivers, cliffs, heavy undergrowth, etc, should be factored in to funnel the enemy into the killing zone. In some cases, it may be necessary to remove some obstructions, either to channel the enemy or to clear a field of fire. Care must be taken when clearing undergrowth or branches that artificial-looking gaps are not left. The ambush party should have good intelligence about enemy travel patterns along a given trail or through an area. It is important to select a site where the enemy will not expect to be ambushed. Fields of fire should be predetermined carefully and weapons sited accordingly.

- **The ambush party should be well concealed.** For an ambush to be successful, the ambush party should remain concealed until the assault is triggered. As a result, care must be taken in selecting and building hides. Radio silence must also be maintained.

- **The ambush party must be determined to wait for the kill.** Members of the team must be patient enough to wait for hours or, in some cases, even days for the enemy to enter their sights. On occasion, it may be necessary to call off the ambush and reset it at another time.

- **There should be a simple plan for launching the ambush.** Normally, the KISS (Keep It Simple, Stupid) principle should apply to launching an ambush. Effective means of initiating the ambush include the detonation of a Claymore mine, a shot from a sniper, or a burst of fire from the man in the best position to determine when every member of the target group has entered the killing zone.

- **There must be good escape routes.** The ambush team should have determined in advance a primary escape route from the ambush site, as well as alternates. Each team member should be well briefed on these routes; in case the team becomes separated, there should also be a predetermined meeting point. If enough personnel are available, teams may be placed to cover escape routes and warn of possible enemy presence. Each member of the ambush party should be trained in tactics for disengagement under fire, and escape and evasion. The escape plan must take into consideration the possibility that at least some members of the ambush team will have been wounded and will need to be carried to a medevac site.

- **There should be a deception plan.** In some cases, a diversion may be used to distract attention from the possibility of an ambush or to draw off possible reinforcements. This is particularly effective if the ambush is being set in an urban environment. Guerrilla/terrorist kidnappings based upon an ambush commonly use a deception plan.

THE URBAN AMBUSH

Carlos Merighela, in his *Minimanual for the Urban Guerrilla*, points out that the guerrilla will have the advantage of surprise, a better knowledge of the terrain, greater speed and mobility, better intelligence and more decisiveness. Note, however, that well trained special-operations units fighting a counter-insurgency campaign will normally have these same advantages when setting ambushes.

Merighela sets out the following steps for carrying out the successful urban ambush:

1 Careful intelligence gathering and analysis.

2 Careful observation of the target. Reconnaissance.

3 Study and timing of routes.

4 Mapping.

5 Transportation.

6 Selection of personnel (this can be a

7 particular problem with guerrillas, many of whom will lack the self-discipline necessary to plan and carry out an effective ambush).

8 Selection of weapons and personnel to use them (another problem for guerrillas, many of whom never have a chance to practise with their weapons).

9 Simulated ambushes (*ie* rehearsals).

10 Execution of the ambush.

11 Cover for those carrying out the ambush.

12 Withdrawal.

13 Removal of the wounded.

14 Destruction of clues.

TYPES OF AMBUSH

Counter-insurgency forces must be versatile in setting ambushes to fit the circumstances and terrain. It is also important to vary the types of ambush used so that the guerrillas will never know what to expect.

Types of ambush include:

- **Linear Ambush.** In this type of ambush, fire is directed from one flank against the enemy. This works particularly well when it is difficult to move off the trail or road because of a height or drop to one side of it.

The disadvantages are that a linear ambush is relatively easy to outflank and more difficult to use against a large force (see *fig. 9.1*).

- **L-Ambush.** In this type, the ambush party takes up positions resembling the letter 'L'. The long side is normally parallel to the enemy's line of march; the short leg is positioned to fire down the enemy column, often with a machine-gun. Claymores or other explosives may be set along the long side of the ambush as well for greater killing effect. In some cases, fire will be held from the short leg of the ambush until the enemy begins to regroup and is used to scatter any possible counterattack (see *fig. 9.2*)

- **V-Ambush.** In this type, the ambush party takes up positions resembling the letter 'V', the two legs meeting at a point in front, or to the rear, of the line of march. The danger, however, is that the ambush party will hit members of their own side in a crossfire; thus, this type of ambush works best if launched from heights where the ambushers can fire down on the enemy (see *fig. 9.3*).

Fig. 9.1. Linear Ambush. Note that a road block has been incorporated to halt the vehicles. The two crew served machine-guns define the killing zone at front and rear.

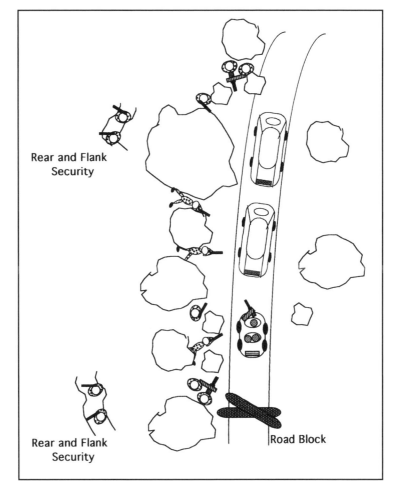

Rear and Flank Security

Rear and Flank Security

Road Block

- **Demolition Ambush.** This type employs explosives and is particularly useful when a small unit sets out to ambush a larger guerrilla force. It is somewhat time consuming to set the explosive devices, so good intelligence about the guerrilla route is needed. Once the explosives have been set, it is important to have one or more observer/flankers in position

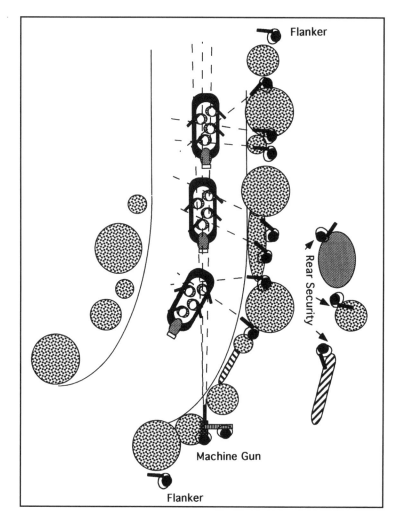

Fig. 9.2. L-Ambush against guerrilla movement on a river.

Flanker

Rear Security

Machine Gun

Flanker

to let the team commander know when the enemy is within the killing zone. Then he can detonate the explosive devices.

- **Bait-Trap Ambush.** This type of ambush is used to increase enemy casualties. It is normally based on knowledge of an enemy's

Fig. 9.3. V-Ambush of a guerrilla pack train. Note that the ambush is set on the high ground to limit the possibility of other members of the ambush team being hit in a crossfire. This is a danger with any ambush, but particularly a V-Ambush. Note also that the belt-fed machine-gun is sited to fire down the length of the pack train, while the ambusher with the rocket launcher is positioned to create panic among the animals in an attempted retreat.

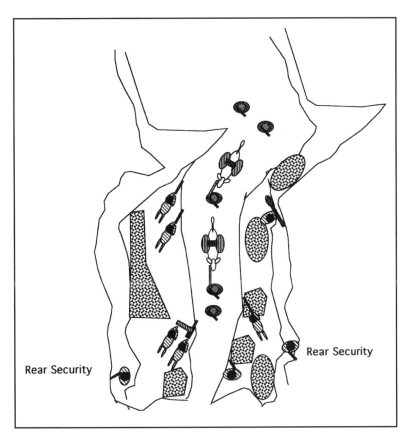

Rear Security

Rear Security

immediate action drills and is designed to turn them against him. For example, a linear ambush may be set so that a ditch appears to offer cover on the side away from the assault; however, detonating cord or other explosives will be placed in the ditch and set off when the enemy takes cover there (see *fig. 9.4*).

• **Pin-Wheel Ambush.** This type of ambush is used when it is unclear from which direction an enemy will approach. The support element will normally be in the centre so that heavy fire can be delivered in any

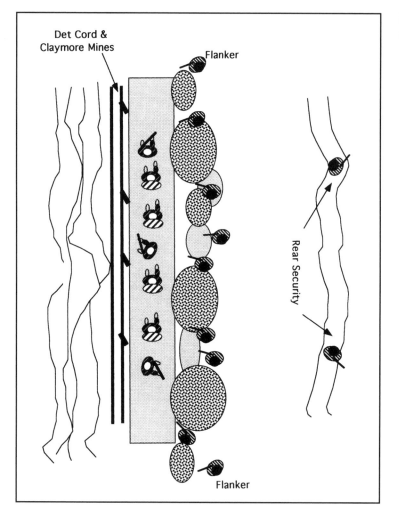

Det Cord &
Claymore Mines

Flanker

Rear Security

Flanker

Fig. 9.4. Linear Bait-Trap Ambush.

direction. This type of ambush is very difficult to control and should only be used when other options are not available. For example, if a recon unit is pursued by a guerrilla force at night, the pin-wheel ambush might be set around the area in which the patrol is resting.

AUTHOR'S NOTE

The general precept is that ambush sites and types should be varied constantly. However, in Afghanistan, ambushes have been the way of war for so many centuries, and the lines of communication through mountain passes are so few, that many of the ambush sites used against Soviet troops were employed by ancestors of the Mujahidin against the British, and probably even against Alexander the Great!

FACTORS GOVERNING SUCCESS

In Afghanistan, the Soviets found ambushes to be their most reliable source of intelligence. This not only illustrates one of the values of ambushes, but also points to the problems that the Soviet Union experienced in developing intelligence sources among a hostile population. By their own admission, however, only about ten per cent of Soviet ambushes

were successful. This lack of success can be attributed to various factors, including their unwillingness to set ambushes at night; their constant use of radios due to a reluctance to vest initiative in junior officers; their tendency to leave litter and to defecate around an ambush site; and their tendency to smoke while in ambush positions.

Counter-insurgency forces must not

COUNTERING GUERRILLA AMBUSHES

only be skilled in setting ambushes, but also at breaking them. It must be borne in mind, for example, that a standard guerrilla tactic is to set ambushes for forces relieving an outpost or unit under attack. An alert lead man, ever watchful for tell-tale signs that a patrol may be walking into an ambush, is one of the best defences against a counter-insurgency unit being ambushed. Trained scout dogs are also invaluable for alerting a unit to a potential ambush. If, however,

Rhodesian troops practise immediate action drills in case of ambush. (*David Scott-Donelan*)

a patrol does walk into a guerrilla ambush, then well-rehearsed immediate action drills can, quite literally, be life savers. The US Army's Ranger Handbook describes immediate action drills as, 'prearranged plans for small units predicated upon swift, aggressive action by each member of the unit.'

BASIC ACTIONS

Other counter-ambush basics are predicated upon when the ambush is discovered. If an alert lead man spots the ambush before any members of

the unit have entered the killing zone, the patrol can choose to retreat or attempt to flank the guerrilla ambush and launch an attack of their own. If some of the unit are caught in the killing zone, they immediately lay down fire on the ambushers and attempt to extricate themselves quickly from the ambush. Those members of the unit not in the killing zone will give covering fire.

Another immediate action drill that is often used is based upon two-man fire teams, who alternate firing and retreating to cover. By leapfrogging in

Fig. 9.5. Drake Shooting Drill for counter-ambush. This drill is designed to allow a unit to immediately engage ambushers, even if their location has not yet been identified. By quickly putting a few rounds into each potential hiding place within his arc of fire, each man can rapidly go on to the offensive and help break an ambush. Note that arcs of fire must be carefully practised to avoid hitting a comrade.

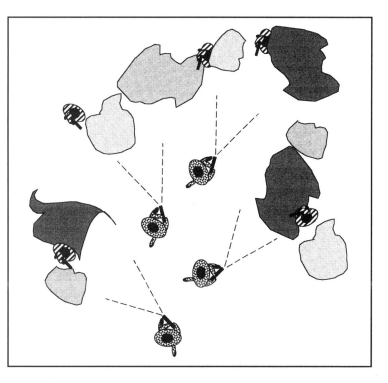

EXAMPLE

One of the most effective immediate action drills for counter-ambush was developed by the Rhodesian counter-insurgency forces and is usually known as the 'Drake Firing Drill'. If a unit comes under fire, the drill requires each member of the unit immediately to place a couple of rounds into any potential hiding place for an attacker within his field of fire. This drill takes substantial practice to carry out smoothly, but when mastered, it allows a patrol to quickly break an ambush without the usual delay caused by determining the source of fire.

this manner, they can quickly extricate themselves while still making it very 'hot' for the enemy. If all members of the patrol have entered the killing zone when the ambush is launched, white phosphorous ('Willie Pete') or fragmentation grenades should be thrown towards guerrilla firing points, followed up by small arms fire. Smoke grenades may also be used to cover a withdrawal or counterattack.

ATTACK THE ATTACKERS

It must be remembered that possible escape routes may well be booby-trapped; thus, the safest course of action in many cases is to attack the ambushers and fight through them. On occasion, it may be possible to flank them, but care must be taken not to put members of the patrol in a crossfire. At all costs, a patrol that faces an ambush must seize the initiative immediately and attempt to achieve fire superiority as soon as possible. Do not become pinned down in the killing zone! Once a guerrilla ambush has been broken, the counter-insurgency force should attempt to

keep the guerrillas on the move while calling for blocking forces to take up

THE VALUE OF BOOBY-TRAPS

positions ahead of them.

Booby-traps are equally useful to the guerrilla and the counter-insurgency soldier. They are frequently deployed along trails to serve three purposes:

1
2

To kill or injure those using the trail.
To slow movement because of the
3 need for extra caution in case booby-traps are encountered.
To lower morale because of the debilitating effect of seeing comrades blown to pieces or impaled on spikes.

Particularly when applied against guerrillas, booby-traps also have the advantage of creating wounded, which insurgent medical services generally have trouble treating in a timely manner. Each wounded guerrilla requires at least two others to carry him, as well as medical personnel to

Guerrillas often use booby-traps to inflict casualties on counter-insurgency forces and loyal members of the population. Here, a track in Vietnam is being checked for mines. (*USMC*)

treat him. Since guerrilla medical services will frequently be more primitive than those of the government, there is a further lowering of morale among guerrillas, who may have to watch comrades die from infection or suffer through lack of proper medication. For these same reasons, security forces often prefer small arms with serious wounding capability rather than killing power. In Vietnam, for example, the .223 bullet of the M-16 rifle may not have had the killing effect of the .308 bullet of the M-14 it replaced, but it created

IMPROVISED BOOBY-TRAPS

numerous casualties.

Guerrillas, particularly, make use of

Counter-insurgency soldiers, such as this member of the US Army Special Forces, must be skilled in bushcraft and creating improvised booby-traps.

improvised booby-traps. In Southeast Asia, the pit filled with *punji* spikes covered in excrement has long been a favourite. So common were this and other types of insurgent penetrative booby-trap in Vietnam, that a special jungle boot with a steel insole was developed for US infantrymen. Other improvised booby-traps have also seen wide use by guerrillas. These include tree branches affixed with sharpened

stakes and pulled back to be released by a trip wire, and a grid of sharpened stakes which are released by a trip wire. One of the simplest guerrilla booby-traps is to release poisonous snakes in latrines and barracks.

Another form of improvised booby-trap has made use of a rifle cartridge buried under a trail with a sharp nail placed beneath the primer to detonate the round when pressure is applied. Special-ops forces have employed a more sophisticated and reliable version of this booby-trap by burying what is, in effect, a single-barrel weapon with a spring-loaded firing pin that is fired when stepped upon.

Special-operations troops operating in guerrilla territory have also used improvised booby-traps, in many cases *punji* stakes, deadfalls or others learned from guerrillas. A popular technique in Vietnam was to nail an empty ration can to a tree at an angle of 30 degrees or so. A fragmentation grenade was placed in the can, with the pin pulled, but the firing lever held down by the sides of the can. A trip wire was stretched across the adjacent trail. Any guerrilla hitting the trip wire would pull the grenade from the can, detonating it. Some US special-ops troops have also learned from assignment on anti-drug operations that fish hooks strung from trees at eye level along a trail can discourage fast pursuit when it is

EXPLOSIVE BOOBY-TRAPS

necessary to E&E (Escape and Evade).

Explosive booby-traps are widely used by both guerrilla and counter-guerrilla forces. US long-range patrols operating in enemy controlled territory, for example, learned to make good use of Claymore mines placed around their positions at night; the Claymore has been widely used by other special-ops personnel against guerrillas. No doubt, captured Claymore mines have been employed by guerrillas as well.

INITIATING DEVICES

Counter-insurgency forces must understand the types of initiating device used to detonate explosive booby-traps to be able to use them

effectively or spot them. Generally, triggers for explosive booby-traps can be divided into two types: Ordnance, which are triggers designed specifically for booby-trapping; and Improvised, which are triggers easily manufactured from available materials. Inexpensive micro-circuitry and mini-detonators have made the task of those setting booby-traps even easier.

For simplicity, booby-trap initiating devices can be categorised into the following types:

• **Ordnance Triggers.** Normally, ordnance triggers or switches depend upon some mechanical means based upon motion to initiate the explosion. These include push switches, activated by direct or indirect application of pressure; pull switches, activated by pressure away from the trigger by a string or a lever; tension release, activated by the sudden release of tension, which had held the trigger 'cocked'; and pressure release, activated by the removal of weight or a restraining mechanism. Note that these types of booby-trap are very widely used to catch counter-insurgency forces searching a village, guerrilla base, etc. Pull switches, for example, can be affixed to the drawers of a desk in an abandoned guerrilla HQ.

- **Elapsed-Time Triggers.** These devices are widely used for acts of sabotage and, therefore, are more likely to be used by guerrillas. Among the types of time delay are lead-and-spring activated, which employs a wire blocked by a soft lead strip that initiates the device when it cuts through the lead; acid-and-spring activated, in which acid eats through a copper wire to release a spring; and chemical time pencil activated, in which a chemical solution corrodes a wire holding a firing pin under tension. An improvised time-delay device can be constructed by placing a grenade in a can of water and putting the can into a freezer until the grenade is frozen in ice. Then the grenade may be removed from the can, placed where it can inflict injuries, and the pin pulled; it will detonate when the ice melts and releases the arming

lever. Of course, inexpensive digital watches are widely employed for timing devices. In fact, the use of Casio watches as timing devices is a trademark of Al-Qaeda.

- **Electric Initiators.** This type of initiator is more sophisticated, but due to the availability of electric components virtually anywhere in the world, it may still be constructed by insurgents. Types include light-sensitive switches, X-ray-sensitive switches, infra-red-sensitive switches, infra-red-beam switches (which detonate a device if a beam is broken), microwave switches, circuit-collapse switches (which operate when power is turned off or a battery runs out), heat-sensitive switches, smoke-sensitive switches, audio-frequency-sensitive switches, vibration-sensitive switches and magnetic switches.
- **Command Detonation.** These devices are set to go off in response to a signal. They include radio-signal initiated devices (model aircraft controls have been widely used), hard-wired devices, altitude devices (triggered by air pressure at a certain

THE USE OF FIRE FOR BOOBY-TRAPS

altitude), and combinations of a radio-signal and other type of trigger. Other simple booby-traps can make use of fire. For example, leaving the gas turned on in a house, then taping matches to a door in such a way that they will strike when the door is opened can create a massive fire bomb. Various field expedient methods have been developed for making napalm, using petroleum, soap/naphtha flakes and shredded

TAILORING BOOBY-TRAPS TO CIRCUMSTANCES

styrene cups. This can form a horrendous, fiery booby-trap. The development of booby-traps in counter-insurgency warfare will often evolve to suit the circumstances of the insurgency. In Malaya, for example, the very effective food control measures implemented by the government caused the MCP to be constantly on the search for supplies; thus, booby-trapped food offered potential gains for

EXAMPLE

An example of the creativity that may be used in constructing booby-traps is illustrated by a Selous Scouts story, related to the author by two veterans of the unit, but which still may be apocryphal. Allegedly, a Selous Scouts pseudo-team believed that they had been compromised and were being lured into an ambush by a group of guerrillas. One of the Scouts, an explosives expert, was said to have constructed an audio detonated device in what appeared to be a 'captured' radio, which he gave to one of the guerrillas to take to the guerrilla leader. The plan was that the guerrilla leader would use the radio to call the pseudo-guerrillas into his camp when ready to receive them (ie when his ambush was ready). When he turned the radio on and called them however – boom!

the security forces. In Vietnam, the tendency of the Viet Cong to cache weapons and ammunition allowed US special-ops forces to seed overloaded ammunition and grenades with instantaneous fuses. Not only did this kill and maim the enemy, but also it undermined his confidence in his weapons. In Northern Ireland, British forces have used scanners that send out radio waves, detonating at least some IRA bombs while being transported or placed. Not only has this destroyed some IRA bombers before they could place their devices, but also it has made them look incompetent in an effective piece of psy-ops. In a way, that is the perfect summation of booby-traps when used by guerrillas or counter-insurgency forces – devices that cause casualties, but that also undermine confidence and morale.

DETECTING BOOBY-TRAPS

Although sophisticated mine detectors/magnetometers may be used to find some types of booby-trap,

counter-insurgency forces patrolling in guerrilla territory, especially small special-ops units, will not be able to carry such equipment. Moreover, many current explosive booby-traps are made without metal components, specifically to make them harder to detect. The Cuban TM D-44 and Russian/Chinese TM D-B mines, for example, have wooden casings and have been widely employed by insurgents. Because of the need to travel lightly, patrols operating in areas where they might expect to encounter booby-traps operated by trip wires often resort to field-expedient detectors. Such a device can be made from a relatively long tree limb or branch, stripped of smaller branches and leaves, with a string and weight attached at one end. It this stick is held in front of the lead man, with the weight just touching the ground, the string will normally snag on any trip wire without detonating the booby-trap.

Because ambushes and booby-traps offer a small force such great potential for inflicting heavy enemy casualties while providing a good chance of escape, they will remain

CHAPTER 10

TRACKERS AND PSEUDO-GUERRILLAS

To destroy insurgents in the field, they must first be found. As a result, skilled trackers have proved invaluable in counter-insurgency campaigns. The SAS, for example, found Iban trackers of great assistance in Malaya and Borneo. In cases such as Borneo, where Indonesian supported Border Terrorists and Indonesian special forces were constantly crossing the border, trackers are necessary to find and eliminate the insurgents. Earlier, during the American Indian Wars, Indian scouts were key elements in US cavalry units hunting the raiding parties. Trackers were considered so important during the Rhodesian counter-insurgency war that a special Tracker Combat Unit was formed, and a school for training trackers was established. In fact, the commander of that school, David Scott-Donelan, continues to train military and police trackers in the USA and around the world. The Portuguese also made extensive use of trackers in Mozambique. Often former FRELIMO guerrillas, these trackers were under the command of a professional hunter.

ESSENTIAL KNOWLEDGE FOR TRACKERS

The counter-guerrilla tracker must be able to follow, interpret, anticipate and react when on the trail of insurgents. To be most effective, he must have a good knowledge of the local terrain.

Trackers should be able to interpret animal and bird behaviour, which often will give an indication of the location of a guerrilla party. This knowledge can also help a tracking team spot an ambush before it can be sprung. They must not only be able to spot hidden guerrillas, but also be skilled themselves at camouflage to avoid detection. Since good trackers employ all of their senses, including the 'sixth sense', part of their training should be drills to sharpen the senses of smell, sight and

Selous Scouts trainees learning tracking and patrolling skills. (*David Scott-Donelan*)

EXAMPLE

In his classic work, *Tactical Tracking Operations*, David Scott-Donelan offers an excellent example of the use of knowledge of the terrain. During the Rhodesian counter-insurgency war, a party of guerrillas was spotted in the Zambezi Valley, travelling towards one of the few water-holes in the foothills of the Zambezi. From knowledge of the area, their destination was deduced and ambushes were set along the trails leading to each water-hole, while trackers were inserted behind the guerrillas. Ambushed each time they attempted to get water, the guerrillas were also stalked by wild animals. Their numbers were thinned even more by tracking teams that trailed them after each ambush. The point is that a good tracker should know water sources, deserted huts, caves and any other features in an area that might attract guerrillas.

hearing. Just as members of patrols operating in enemy territory avoid the use of soap, shaving lotion, deodorant and other toiletries, which will produce tell-tale odours, so should the tracker, preventing the betrayal of his presence to an enemy skilled in bushcraft.

FOLLOWING A TRAIL

When in pursuit of guerrillas, the tracker looks for four main indicators:

1 Ground spoor. Marks or imprints left on the ground (*ie* footprints).

2 Aerial spoor. Damage to vegetation left by the passage of the guerrillas. To a skilled tracker, aerial spoor can often indicate direction and time (*ie* displaced grass, twigs, branches, etc, will normally point in the direction of movement); moss scraped from trees, broken spiders' webs and myriad other anomalies offer the skilled tracker clues to the guerrillas' route.

3 Sign. This includes a variety of other miscellaneous indicators, including stones that have been displaced, overturned leaves, scuff marks on rocks or trees, etc.

Litter. Items left behind on the trail, in

4 camp, etc.

When following spoor, a good tracker will be able to estimate its age and the effects of weather, or human or animal actions upon it.

David Scott-Donelan offers the following rules for counter-guerrilla trackers:

Identify the correct tracks to follow.

1 Mark the point where tracking begins

2 (in case it is necessary to backtrack, or the trail is lost and it is necessary to start again).

Do not walk on top of the spoor.

3 Do not overshoot the last known spoor.

4 When following aerial spoor or sign,

5 check for additional confirmable evidence.

The tracker should remain aware of his

6 location at all times.

Stay in visual contact with other

7 members of the tracking team.

Attempt to anticipate what the guerrilla

8 being tracked will do.

LOST SPOOR

If the spoor is lost, there are two basic procedures:

1 Return to the last known spoor and extrapolate a likely continuation. Check for indications that the guerrillas have taken that route, but if not, try the next most likely continuation.

2 Move backwards a distance and begin circling the last known spoor, searching for any indications of passage by the guerrilla force.

At times, it will also be valuable to backtrack along the guerrillas' trail to discover its starting point. This might allow guerrilla infiltration points to be discovered or help identify a site being reconnoitred for possible guerrilla attack.

ESSENTIAL ACTIONS

When on the track of a guerrilla party, David Scott-Donelan advises the following:

1 Determine the correct spoor.

2 Determine the number of guerrillas being tracked.

3 Note their footwear or other distinguishing characteristics.

4 Determine the initial direction of movement.

5 Determine the age of the spoor or sign.

6 Attempt to obtain a description of the guerrillas and any other useful information about them, including how they are armed.

7 If possible, determine any past operations or contacts of this particular guerrilla group to learn something about their tactics.

8 Determine whether the guerrillas have been known to use anti-tracking methods.

THE TRACKING TEAM

In counter-guerrilla tracking, a four-man team is the norm. This allows the team to protect itself more effectively against ambush and to follow up a contact. It also helps prevent fatigue, since team members can take turns at the tracking task; thus, a team can travel faster and farther. Extra eyes and ears also allow lost spoor to be located more quickly and the faster gathering of intelligence, especially aerial spoor. Overall, the tracking team offers more versatility. The four-man group has the additional advantage of fitting well into many special-operations units that use the four-man team as a basic element.

Within the four-man team, functions are broken down as follows:

- **Controller.** In charge of communication, maintains visual contact with other team members, usually responsible for marking the last known spoor.
- **Tracker.** Actually follows the spoor.
- **Left and Right Flankers.** Move slightly ahead of the tracker on the flanks, providing flank security and watching for ambushes or booby-traps; also help search for lost spoor when necessary.

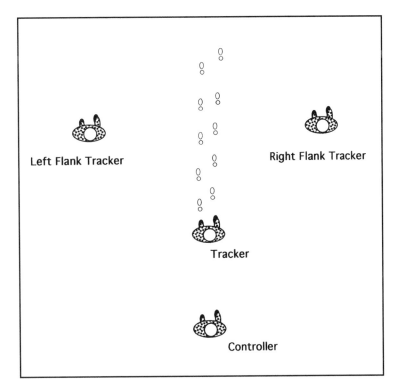

Fig. 10.1. Y Tracking Formation.

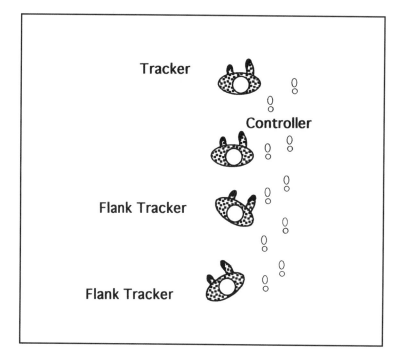

Tracker

Controller

Flank Tracker

Flank Tracker

Left, fig. 10.2. Single-File Tracking Formation. This formation is for use in heavy bush, where it would be difficult for flank trackers to keep up in a standard formation.

Facing page, fig. 10.3. Extended-Line Tracking Formation. This formation is useful on relatively clear terrain where the spoor may be difficult to spot.

TRACKING FORMATION

The standard tracking formation is the 'Y' (see *fig. 10.1*), but other formations (*figs. 10.2* and *10.3*), including single-file for thick brush, may be used. To maintain noise discipline, the tracking team will normally employ hand signals. The trackers may be followed by support teams in case of contact with large guerrilla groups. However, these support teams must be composed of highly trained light infantry to keep up with the trackers.

IMMEDIATE ACTION DRILLS
The tracking team must have prepared immediate action drills, based on three possible scenarios:

1 The tracking team sees the guerrillas first.

2 The tracking team and guerrillas see each other simultaneously.

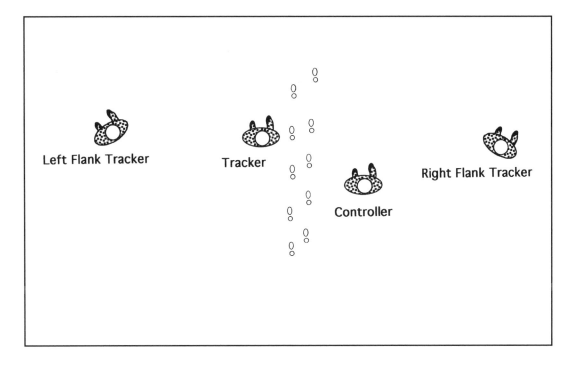

Left Flank Tracker

Tracker

Controller

Right Flank Tracker

3 The tracking team is ambushed by hidden guerrillas.

OTHER TYPES OF TRACKING UNIT

Although trackers on foot have proved most effective in counter-guerrilla operations, other types of tracking unit have also been employed successfully. Aerial tracking, for example, has proved valuable, especially in very open, arid country, where footprints may be visible from the air. In Rhodesia, Grey's Scouts, a mounted infantry unit, used trackers on horseback, although normally they would dismount to read sign or spoor. The horses' height offered the advantage of extending their riders' field of view when looking for sign or attempting to spot guerrillas in the distance.

Mounted trackers can cover greater distances with less fatigue, have a psychological effect on those being pursued, can carry more equipment and can launch an assault quickly if the guerrillas are spotted. However, horses need a great deal of water, so the area of operations must have abundant water sources. Mounted trackers are also likely to require aerial re-supply at some point. Horses tend to be afraid of fire, and they will have to be well trained not to flinch when firearms are used. They are noisy too, making it more difficult to approach guerrillas in a stealthy manner. A mounted tracking unit will require special transport to move its animals to an area of operations. Among other disadvantages are that horses will not be able to move well in heavy brush, jungle or forest; will be susceptible to flies and other insects; and will require veterinary and blacksmith support. Finally, a horse and rider make more visible targets for an ambush. Interestingly, however, the Grey's Scouts camouflaged their horses so well that few were lost to enemy fire.

Vehicle-borne trackers have proved effective in open country. In Namibia, for example, the South West African Police counter-insurgency teams found that the flat, barren terrain lent itself to the use of trackers in off-road vehicles. These vehicles carried a driver, gunner and twelve native police trackers. They would patrol looking for sign, and when any was found would dismount the trackers to follow it up, engaging any guerrillas encountered with the firepower carried on the vehicle.

USE OF DOGS

Tracker dogs have also been used successfully in counter-guerrilla operations. They are particularly valuable for short-range tracking and for finding the initial trail, which then can be followed up by human trackers. Since dogs track by scent rather than sight, they will usually be more effective at night than human trackers. Dogs are also especially useful against guerrillas who are running, since they will leave a sharper scent trail. On longer tracking operations, however, dogs are normally less efficient, as they become

Dogs have been used extensively in counter-insurgency campaigns; in this case by the USAF Security Police to protect an air base in Vietnam. (*USAF*)

tired. Their handlers will need to carry extra food and water for them as well. Additionally, good tracking dogs need specialised training.

One of the greatest values of dogs is their ability to alert their human companions to ambushes and, in some cases, booby-traps. However, they must be trained for scouting as well as tracking to be effective members of a patrol.

COUNTER-TRACKING TECHNIQUES

Tracking teams must be familiar with the techniques guerrillas use to confuse trackers, and understand how to compensate for counter-tracking techniques. On the other hand, trackers and special-operations troops need to know how to counter trackers in case they find themselves operating in guerrilla controlled areas and subject to being tracked themselves.

In general, four main techniques are used to counter trackers:

1 **Moving fast to outdistance the trackers.** Although this method has been used successfully to elude trackers, especially if a safe haven such as a border is nearby, normally the guerrillas will leave more easily discernible spoor by hurrying and will actually make the job of tracking them easier. As mentioned previously, this makes it relatively easy for dogs to track the guerrillas.

2 **Concealing spoor.** Various techniques have been employed to conceal guerrilla spoor, with greater or lesser degrees of success. One of the most common is to brush out tracks with branches or even a broom. However, unless such

brushing is carried out very carefully, which will slow the guerrillas substantially, the brush marks may actually be easier to follow than would have been the original spoor. Another technique is to replace vegetation that has been displaced, but this does not remove any ground spoor. Moving over rocky or hard ground is effective, but a skilled tracker may still be able to pick up the trail by searching for sign. A common method is to walk in stream beds; in this case, the tracker must simply follow the stream looking for the point at which the guerrillas left it. Changing footwear has been used to good effect, although unless it is done at a point where many footprints converge, this ploy may still be obvious. Fallen trees have been employed as walkways, and guerrillas have stepped from rock to rock in an attempt to confuse trackers, but usually scuff marks, mud or other traces will be left – or the tracker may pick up the trail when the guerrilla returns to the ground. Walking on a well-travelled path may confuse the tracker, but once again, he can regain the spoor by looking for the point at which the guerrilla leaves the path. Walking backwards is actually one of the easiest ruses to detect, since the skilled tracker can recognise the difference in the primary impact marks this causes. One of the most confusing methods of countering the tracker is to make sudden changes of direction, which will certainly slow even skilled trackers.

3 **Spoor reduction.** This technique has been widely used by guerrilla groups, particularly if they are local insurgent 'militia' who return to their villages after operations. One of the appeals of this technique is that it is very simple and often effective. As a guerrilla party moves along, one or two members at a time split off, especially when moving over hard or rocky ground, where their departure will be difficult to detect.

4 **Counter-tracking.** This is the most aggressive method of countering trackers, as it actually entails attacking the trackers through the use of booby-traps, mines or ambushes. If successful, this tactic has the advantage for the guerrillas

of reducing the number of trackers, slowing them down, having a psychological impact and, in the case of explosive booby-traps, marking their location for the guerrillas. Even if booby-traps or mines do not injure or kill any of the trackers, they will slow pursuit, as the tracking team must spend time watching for additional traps.

TRACKERS' EQUIPMENT

Although the tracker will want to travel as lightly as possible, he must be prepared to engage the enemy and, thus, needs a rifle, shotgun or submachine-gun, backed up by a handgun. He will also need a good combat knife, binoculars, compass, water bottles, spare ammunition, rain gear, medical kit and rations; sleeping gear will be required on long missions. The controller will have the team radio.

HIGH-TECH AIDS
There are a few high-tech devices that can also be invaluable to the tracker.

The GPS speeds the operation, since the tracker will not have to make regular stops to consult a map and/or compass, although a compass should still be carried as a back-up to the GPS. Current military GPS units are so accurate that positions such as the start point of the track, possible spoor-reduction split-off points, locations of booby-traps or mines for future EOD (Explosive Ordnance Disposal) follow-up, etc, may be entered for later use. The GPS, which gives the team's position in longitude and latitude, may also be used to guide in reinforcements if needed.

Although a sight tracker will normally not be able to track at night except, perhaps, in bright moonlight, infra-red or other night-vision optics will prove valuable in darkness, especially when approaching the guerrilla force. Sound enhancement devices, which allow the tracker to hear footsteps out to a distance of 1000 metres, are also quite useful. As with any mission where troops must carry everything themselves, each piece of equipment must be evaluated on a utility-versus-weight-and-bulk basis.

TRAINING TRACKERS

Tracking teams require substantial training and experience to be effective, but once good trackers are available, the pursuit and elimination of guerrilla bands become much easier. Frequently, reliance is put on indigenous trackers, many of whom are excellent and have the advantage of intimate knowledge of the terrain. However, it will also be valuable to train as trackers members of special-operations forces who may be assigned to counter-insurgency duties. Additionally, anyone who may work with indigenous trackers needs at least a basic knowledge of tracking to be able to interpret the information gained by them, and also to be able to make a decision if trackers offer several interpretations of sign or spoor.

PSEUDO-GUERRILLA OPERATIONS

Because trackers are at home in rough country, in some cases, they have also

Pseudo-guerrilla forces are often formed from guerrillas who have been turned. (*David Scott-Donelan*)

been tasked with cross-border operations and pseudo-guerrilla missions. Pseudo-guerrilla groups are generally formed from turned insurgents, on occasion combined with local military personnel or even whites in 'black face' (as in Kenya and Rhodesia). Such groups can be useful for gathering intelligence, as they can exchange 'gossip' with real guerrilla groups, but they are most useful for getting close to guerrilla units, then ambushing them. Multi-cultural societies, such as the USA, Great Britain and Russia, often have special forces personnel of myriad racial and ethnic types who can blend with a pseudo-group as well.

PSEUDO-GUERRILLAS IN HISTORY

Pseudo-guerrillas have been used to good effect in insurgencies for more than a century. In the Philippine Insurrection at the turn of the twentieth century, for example, a pseudo-guerrilla unit bringing in American 'prisoners' was used to get near an insurgent leader so that he could be killed or captured. Once again in the Philippines, Force X was a pseudo-force used against the Huks. Force X proved particularly effective in identifying village leaders who collaborated with the Huks. The group's 'guerrillas' were also 'captured' by the police and imprisoned with other Huks from whom they gathered valuable intelligence. In Malaya, Q-Force Penang was formed in 1952 from captured CTs (Communist Terrorists). In 1953, the programme was expanded to the Special Operations Volunteer Force. However, other methods, such as population and resource controls, proved so successful that eventually the pseudo-groups were phased out.

Pseudo-operations were more successful in Kenya, where turned Mau Mau gangsters mixed with loyal Kikuyu, and white police and military personnel in 'black face' were used to form pseudo-gangs, whose primary targets were the Mau Mau leaders. The whites did find it necessary also to blacken their bodies in case their shirts were lifted, and some even constructed wigs from the hair of killed Mau Mau. Since real Mau Mau tended to call at villages at night, the pseudo-gangs operated primarily at night as well, a fact that helped white members pass for Mau Mau. Frank Kitson, who had initiated the pseudo-programme, eventually set up the Special Methods Training Centre for pseudo-operators in June 1954. Every attempt was made to give authenticity to pseudo-gangs, including allowing girlfriends and wives to accompany the 'gangsters'.

Facing page: Rhodesia's Selous Scouts were extremely effective. Note that this white Scout wears a heavy beard to cover as much of his face as possible. (*David Scott-Donelan*)

Left: Pseudo-guerrilla in Rhodesia.
(*David Scott-Donelan*)

Facing page: Members of the Selous Scouts learning to fire guerrilla weapons.
(*David Scott-Donelan*)

The pseudo-gangs worked especially well in Kenya because of the poor communication between different gangs, making it much more difficult for the Mau Mau to tell friend from foe. In fact, by 1956, pseudo-gangs had become so effective that they were accounting for an average of twenty-two Mau Mau per week. The biggest problem in Kenya and in other places where pseudo-gangs have been used was to keep a constant

Perhaps one of the best examples of the potential effectiveness of pseudo-units was demonstrated by Rhodesia's Selous Scouts. Although they retained the tracking mission they had inherited from the Tracker Combat Unit, the Selous Scouts were particularly effective at pseudo-operations. So successful were they at maintaining a constant influx of turned terrorists that Selous Scouts pseudo-units were often more up to date on terrorist identification procedures and operations than the groups they were infiltrating. Selous Scouts used their ability to pass as members of ZIPRA and ZANLA to carry out assassinations and snatches of key personnel across Rhodesia's borders in guerrilla 'safe areas'. They were also particularly good at gathering intelligence from captured guerrilla diaries and letters.

In addition, Selous Scouts used the ploy of infiltrating guerrilla camps with 'white prisoners'. Audacity was a key element in their successes. In one operation, for example, eighty-four Selous Scouts penetrated into Mozambique and killed over 1000 ZANLA guerrillas

influx of new turned insurgents so that the pseudos could be kept up to date on guerrilla practices, passwords, etc.

Pseudo-guerrillas were used to some extent in Aden, where dark-skinned members of the SAS, including Fijins, dressed as Arabs to mingle in bazaars and watch for wanted guerrillas, or attacks on British personnel or their families. The *firqats* in Oman sometimes functioned as pseudo-gangs, although this was not their primary mission. The Portuguese employed pseudo-guerrillas to some while suffering only five slightly wounded themselves. One of the greatest effects they had upon the guerrillas was psychological. So afraid were many guerrillas of being infiltrated by the Scouts that they would get into fire fights with other guerrilla groups, believing them to be Selous Scouts! One of the Scouts' greatest weapons was the fear and distrust they sewed among their enemies.

To establish their guerrilla credentials, the Selous Scouts would sometimes stage mock raids on farms or assassinations of British South Africa Police informers. As a result, some of their pseudo-units became legendary among the guerrillas for their effectiveness! Because the Scouts were so good at passing themselves off as terrorists, they were often in more danger from the Rhodesian security forces than from ZIPRA or ZANLA. Consequently, the policy was implemented of declaring 'frozen' any area in which the Scouts were operating, and no other Rhodesian security forces were allowed to enter the area until the Scouts had completed their mission.

extent in Angola as well. In the Philippines, a few turned Huks were mixed with members of long-range patrol units and on occasion took part in pseudo-operations.

As with many aspects of counter-insurgency warfare, successful tracking and pseudo-operations will depend on retaining the loyalty of substantial portions of the population, especially in rural areas, and on winning over former guerrillas to the government cause.

CHAPTER 11

CONCLUSIONS

So far, this work has dealt with fairly specific strategies and tactics for dealing with an insurgency. However, it is important to make these specifics part of a general plan for winning a counter-insurgency campaign. First, it must be remembered that a successful counter-insurgency campaign will be waged on at least two levels – governmental and military. Victory must be gained at both levels to truly defeat the insurgency. Since civil officials and military officers may view success in different ways, and since they will often pursue what they perceive as their own route to victory, it is highly advisable to have a unified command for civil and military authorities during a counter-insurgency war. This unified command must establish very clear military and political goals.

WINNING OVER THE POPULATION

One of the first goals of the unified command must be to win the population away from the guerrillas. Attention must be paid, particularly, to minorities or any underclass who may feel disenfranchised. This can be done in many ways, including replacing corrupt or incompetent officials, passing fair laws, equalising educational and employment opportunities, and making life better through medical civic action programmes. It is also crucial to protect loyal members of the population from guerrilla intimidation. Many insurgencies start in rural areas; so it is important to offer assistance in agriculture and husbandry.

Insurgencies stand a far better chance of success if they are nationalistic and are launched against an unpopular government. As a result, it is important to counter guerrilla propaganda with effective psychological operations stressing the government's concerns for the people and pointing out guerrilla shortcomings. Psy-ops that include amnesties to attract less committed guerrillas have proved quite effective in many insurgencies. Religion can also play a role in insurgencies, as in

Cyprus, Northern Ireland, Palestine and Afghanistan. In the case of Afghanistan, where Muslim warriors were fighting the 'godless Communists', the battle lines were clearly drawn and no amount of psy-ops would have made a difference. In other cases, religious tolerance can help blunt the guerrillas' appeal.

It may be necessary to implement measures to separate the population from the guerrillas, including resettlement, resource control, free fire areas and ID cards. For these to work, an effort must be made to show the population that they are designed to protect the people, not oppress them. Intelligence is absolutely crucial in locating and destroying insurgents. A population that supports the counter-insurgency campaign can often be the best source of this intelligence.

TAILORING THE COUNTER-INSURGENCY EFFORT

Insurgents who have outside support, especially if located on a continuous border, have a great advantage. As a result, it may be necessary to devote substantial resources to border control. Diplomatic pressure and, in some cases, military pressure may be necessary to counter such support.

The military counter-insurgency effort must be tailored to fighting guerrillas rather than fighting a conventional war. As a result, emphasis must be placed on light infantry, which can move fast and penetrate into areas where the guerrillas might feel safe. Backing up deep-penetration patrols should be highly mobile reserves, especially air-mobile units. Using conscripts or troops attuned to conventional warfare is also dangerous, as it increases the likelihood of atrocities, because telling friend from foe in a guerrilla war is often difficult. To protect the population and allow them to become more involved in their own defence, hamlet militias and other local defence forces may be formed, often with special forces teams as advisors who live with them. For operations and tracking in remote areas, indigenous tribes can be recruited as a counter-guerrilla force.

171

THE WILL TO WIN

Much of the counter-insurgency effort will be geared to increasing pressure on the guerrillas who, by the nature of their already stressful lifestyle, must maintain a high degree of commitment to their cause. If the guerrillas are constantly harried and kept moving, as well as deprived of their sources of food and recruits, they will be forced to spend time worrying about the basics of life, rather than planning operations against the government and population. Since they lead a life on the run, guerrillas are also prone to paranoia; thus, black psy-ops and pseudo-operations, which cause them to distrust members of their own movement, can sap their will to fight or cause them to consider switching to the government side.

Most of all, while working to sap the guerrillas' will to carry on, government troops must maintain their own will to win. This is one reason why it is far better for a counter-insurgency campaign to be fought by professional soldiers, rather than conscripts, especially when a major power is supporting a developing country with military assistance. The USA found in Vietnam, and the Soviets in Afghanistan, that conscript troops who had little commitment to the campaign were not particularly effective. Support at home for a counter-insurgency war overseas will wane much faster too, if sons conscripted to the war effort start returning home in body bags.

Victory in counter-insurgency warfare is often based on who blinks first, and it must not be the government. Particularly in counter-insurgency campaigns involving major powers propping up 'client' states or colonies, when the guerrillas have been willing to absorb punishment to a much greater extent – as in Indochina, Vietnam and Afghanistan – the major powers have eventually tired of the campaign and pulled out.

RECOMMENDED READING

Advisor Handbook for Stability Operations, FM31-73 (Washington, DC: HQ, Department of the Army, 1967)

An Infantryman's Guide to Urban Combat, FM 90-10-1 (Washington, DC: HQ, Department of the Army, 1982)

Beckett, Ian F.W., *Encyclopedia of Guerrilla Warfare* (Oxford: ABC CLIO, 2000)

Beckett, Ian F.W., *Modern Insurgencies and Counter-Insurgencies: Guerrillas and Their Opponents since 1750* (London: Routledge, 2001)

Callwell, Col. C.E., *Small Wars: A Tactical Textbook for Imperial Soldiers* (London: Greenhill Books, 1990)

Chaliand, Gerard, ed., *Guerrilla Strategies: An Historical Anthology from the Long March to Afghanistan* (Berkeley: University of California Press, 1982)

Counterguerrilla Operations, FM31-16 (Washington, DC: HQ, Department of the Army, 1967)

Grau, Lester W., ed., *The Bear Went Over the Mountain: Soviet Combat Tactics in Afghanistan* (London: Frank Cass, 1998)

Grau, Lester W., ed., *The Soviet-Afghan War: How a Superpower Fought and Lost* (Lawrence: University of Kansas Press, 2002)

Gwynn, Maj.-Gen. Sir Charles, *Imperial Policing* (London: Macmillan, 1936)

Harclerode, Peter, *Fighting Dirty: The Inside Story of Covert Operations from Ho Chi Minh to Osama Bin Laden* (London: Cassell, 2001)

Insurgent War: Selected Case Studies, RB31-100, Vol. II (Fort Leavenworth, KS: US Army Command and General Staff College, 1969)

Jalali, Ali Ahmad, and Grau, Lester W., *Afghan Guerrilla Warfare: In the Words of the Mujahidin Fighters* (St Paul, MN: MBI Publishing, 2001)

Latimore, John, *Deception in War* (Woodstock: The Overlook Press, 2001)

O'Neill, Bard E., *Insurgency and Terrorism: Inside Modern Revolutionary Warfare* (Washington, DC: Brasseys (USA) Inc., 1990)

Paget, Julian, *Counterinsurgency Operations: Techniques of Guerrilla Warfare* (New York: Walker & Company, 1967)

Patrolling and Tracking (Australian Military Force Manual. Boulder, CO: Paladin Press)

Plaster, John, *The Ultimate Sniper* (Boulder, CO: Paladin Press, 1993)

Psychological Operations: Techniques and Procedures, FM33-5 (Washington, DC: HQ, Department of the Army, 1966)

Ranger Handbook (Fort Benning, GA: US Army Infantry School, 1972)

Scott-Donelan, David, *Tactical Tracking Operations* (Boulder, CO: Paladin Press, 1998) For information about tracker training: mantrack@aol.com

Special Forces Handbook, ST31-180 (Washington, DC: HQ, Department of the Army, 1965)

Special Forces Operational Techniques, FM 31-20 (Washington, DC: HQ, Department of the Army, 1965)

Special Forces Operations, FM 31-21 (Washington, DC: HQ, Department of the Army, 1965)

Stubblefield, Gary, and Monday, Mark, *Killing Zone: A Professional's Guide to Preparing or Preventing Ambushes* (Boulder, CO: Paladin Press, 1994)

Terrorist Weapons and Explosives (Boise, ID: Security Awareness and Promotions, 1988)

Thompson, Leroy, *Dirty Wars: Elite Forces Versus the Guerrillas* (Newton Abbot: David & Charles, 1988)

Thompson, Leroy, *Ragged War: The Story of Unconventional and Counter-Revolutionary Warfare* (London: Arms & Armour, 1994)

U.S. Army Counterinsurgency Forces, FM 31-22 (Washington, DC: HQ, Department of the Army, 1963)

Younghusband, Francis, *Indian Frontier Warfare* (London: Kegan, Paul, 1898)

Yousaf, Mohammad, and Adkin, Mark, *Afghanistan, The Bear Trap: The Defeat of a Superpower* (Barnsley: Pen and Sword, 1992)

INDEX